The Crisis of Younger Clergy

More praise for *The Crisis of Younger Clergy*:

"This is not just a book for younger clergy. This is a book for the whole church. It is a book about possibility, potential, and opportunity. This is a book for everyone who cares passionately about our church—its future, its vitality, and its mission."

—Patricia Farris, Senior Minister,
Santa Monica First United Methodist Church

"From statistical analysis to anecdotes from young clergy blogs, [this] detailed picture of the current crisis provides a crucial diagnosis which the church can now use to take constructive action."

—Andrew C. Thompson, young clergy elder and
"Gen X Rising" columnist for the *United Methodist Reporter*

The Crisis of Younger Clergy

LOVETT H. WEEMS JR. AND ANN A. MICHEL

Abingdon Press
Nashville

THE CRISIS OF YOUNGER CLERGY

This book is printed on acid-free paper.

Library of Congress Cataloging-in-Publication Data

Weems, Lovett H. (Lovett Hayes)
The crisis of younger clergy / Lovett H. Weems, Jr. and Ann A. Michel.
p. cm.
ISBN 978-0-687-65109-2 (alk. paper)
1. Clergy—Appointment, call, and election. 2. Vocation, Ecclesiastical. I. Michel, Ann A. II. Title.

BV4011.4.W44 2008
253′.20842—dc222

2008000425

08 09 10 11 12 13 14 15 16 17—10 9 8 7 6 5 4 3 2 1

MANUFACTURED IN THE UNITED STATES OF AMERICA

Contents

Introduction

It is evident that no society … can hold together and can realize great objects without thoroughly qualified leaders. The Church of Christ is no exception. Wherever the Church has proved inadequate it has been due to inadequate leadership.[1]
John R. Mott

In March 2006, the Lewis Center for Church Leadership published a report entitled *Clergy Age Trends in the United Methodist Church: 1985–2005*. The report documented a dramatic drop in the number and percentage of United Methodist clergy under the age of 35 in the last 20 years in the United States. Anyone observing the sea of gray at denominational events could have guessed this to be the case, but there were no firm numbers to document the trend. Unfortunately, the dimensions of the problem proved even worse than one might have guessed. In the United Methodist Church and many other denominations, the percentage of clergy under the age of 35 has dropped to below 5 percent.

The publication of *Clergy Age Trends* was like the sounding of an alarm. It sparked considerable discussion and debate, both within the church and in the mainstream media, about the growing challenge of finding younger persons to lead congregations. In the weeks and months following the release of the clergy age data, the *Atlanta Constitution*, the Associated Press, PBS's *Religion and Ethics Newsweekly*, and NBC's *Today Show* featured reports on the young clergy situation.

What has emerged from this study and other research is an understanding of the young clergy crisis as a complex, multidimensional phenomenon. There is no single cause and no single solution. Among the many factors involved are seminary culture, candidacy procedures, the probationary process, appointment practices, financial considerations, support structures, enlistment efforts, the presence of youth and young adults in congregations, and ageism. Ultimately, however, the issue of enlisting younger clergy must be seen side by side with the quality and vitality of the church itself.

The church's overall health is among the most important factors determining who is likely to respond to the call into ordained ministry. God calls at all times, and people respond to God's call. But it is more likely that God's call will be heard and accepted by more young people if the church is one where they are active and where God's mission to make disciples and transform the world is alive. And arguably, those who enter ordained ministry are among the most important factors determining the overall health of the church. Because the future of the church is linked inextricably with the presence of capable young clergy, this is an issue of extreme importance.

A number of questions surfaced in the discussion. Why do young clergy matter? What challenges do younger clergy face? Why is the number of young clergy declining? And, perhaps most important, what can be done? These and other questions will be addressed in the chapters that follow. The first three chapters of this book describe the nature of the young clergy problem. They outline the scope of the problem, profile the young clergy population, and consider the importance of young clergy. The remaining chapters discuss in greater depth some of the issues and considerations related to the problem. These include specific policies and procedures, such as enlistment, candidacy, and ordination processes; appointment practices; and salary and educational debts. But in the final analysis, these issues are secondary to others that are less tangible *and* less amenable to change: the overall health of the church and its attractiveness to young leaders; the vitality of youth ministry and its effectiveness in cultivating the call among young persons; and the receptivity of church culture to young leaders and new ideas. One young pastor has summarized the essence of the problem in this way: "[T]he ministries of the church are not offering the gospel in ways that are compelling to the hearts and minds of younger adults. Those younger adults who do 'hear the call' to ministry within the United Methodist Church struggle to make sense of their role within an ailing denomination that seems unable or unwilling to minister to the needs of their generation."[2]

The Lewis Center for Church Leadership has explored this subject using a variety of information-gathering methods. Part of this inquiry has involved taking the pulse of younger clergy to learn about their experiences in ministry and to listen to what they say about their standing in the church. In March 2007, the Lewis Center conducted a major survey of United Methodist clergy under 35 to gather data on when and why younger persons enter ministry; factors influencing their decisions; perceptions of how age influences their standing in the church; the nature of their appointments; their financial well-being; and their level of satisfaction in ministry. Almost half of the under-35 elders in The United Methodist Church responded to this survey. This extraordinary response rate indicates the eagerness of young clergy to voice their opinions on these subjects. The blogs of young clergy have provided another window into the world inhabited by young pastors.

The Lewis Center's ongoing leadership development work with those entering ministry has afforded many opportunities for one-on-one conversations and structured focus groups. Also, as the Lewis Center staff has reported the clergy age findings to many different church audiences, there have been opportunities for dialogue with pastors, denominational leaders, church agency personnel, and denominational pension administrators. Their perspectives and feedback have provided an abundance of information as well. Much of the information and many of the quotations in this book are drawn from these conversations or from questionnaires distributed at various gatherings.

This research focused on United Methodism in the United States, and the book deals primarily with United Methodist elders because they constitute the largest category of United Methodist clergy. Ordained deacons as they now exist in The United Methodist Church are relatively new, making trend comparisons difficult. And local pastors have traditionally had an older average age than elders. Therefore, unless otherwise noted, the statistics and information in this book refer only to elders. To have comparable figures across the years, elders are defined for the purposes of this work as not only those who have been ordained elder but also those who have been commissioned on the elder track but are not yet ordained.

We have, however, learned a great deal about young deacons and local pastors as well. Chapter 2 profiles the young clergy population and provides some basic information on how deacons and local pastors fit into the larger young clergy picture. Those interested in more detailed information on deacons and local pastors should consult *Clergy Age Trends in The United Methodist Church: 1985–2005* and other information available at www.church leadership.com.

Although this book focuses primarily on The United Methodist Church, available data on clergy age trends in other denominations also are presented in chapter 1. These data indicate that the decline in young clergy in The United Methodist Church is typical of what is happening in many other North American denominations. Thus, the analysis of young clergy in The United Methodist Church is offered as a case study of a problem that has broad ecumenical implications.

The purpose of this study has been to facilitate learning and dialogue on this critical concern. While we believe our research has made a contribution toward that end, many questions remain unanswered and other new questions have arisen. Such questions point to the need for additional, and more extensive, research. Our purpose here is to interpret to the church at large what we have learned about and from young clergy, though we do not speak *for* them. We are seeking to name realities that, while not universally true among all young clergy and across all conferences, are present for much of the denomination.

Before moving into this discussion, it is important to name and thank those individuals and groups who have made our work possible. First, we wish to thank Abingdon Press and senior editor Robert Ratcliff, who approached us about the possibility of writing this book in order to share more widely what we are learning about young clergy.

We are also grateful to the Lilly Endowment, Inc., particularly for their Transitions into Ministry and Sustaining Pastoral Excellence Initiatives that have helped many denominations, judicatories, and seminaries begin efforts to support the development of a new generation of leaders. Lilly support has permitted Wesley Theological Seminary and the Lewis Center for Church Leadership to develop the Lewis Fellows program for young clergy, study the United Methodist probationary process, and develop cooperative work among conferences to help clergy in their early years of ministry. Craig Dykstra and John Wimmer have been wise guides and encouragers for our work and that of many others.

The help and cooperation of the General Board of Pension and Health Benefits of The United Methodist Church has been essential in documenting age trends among United Methodist clergy. They prepared the historical data for the years 1985–2005 and now provide updated figures annually so that we can help the church monitor clergy age trends. We thank Barbara Boigegrain, the general secretary of the Board, and Anne Borish, Peter Doheny, and Otisstean Arrington of the staff, for vital information and expertise. Thanks go also to The General Council on Finance and Administration for sharing data they collect and to administrators and staff from other denominations for data on age trends in their churches. We have valued the collaboration of The General Board of Higher Education and Ministry with our work, given their efforts around enlistment and overall clergy issues.

Barbara G. Wheeler and Anthony T. Ruger, of the Center for the Study of Theological Education at Auburn Theological Seminary, provided valuable information drawn from their extensive research with seminarians. Likewise, the Association of Theological Schools in the United States and Canada through Daniel O. Aleshire and Chris A. Meinzer provided significant data.

We are indebted to those who made possible the establishment of the Lewis Center for Church Leadership and those who continue to support its work: the Center's Steering Committee and Advisors who, along with faculty and other leaders in the Wesley Theological Seminary community, have guided our work, especially President David McAllister-Wilson and former President G. Douglass Lewis.

Joseph E. Arnold, research manager for the Lewis Center, has been responsible for all the statistical compilations and research that went into this volume and *Clergy Age Trends in The United Methodist Church: 1985–2005*. Joe is a passionate curator of information about the church that he loves. We also thank other members of the Lewis Center staff—Asa J. Lee and Dottie Yunger for research and editorial support, and Frenika Mudd for administrative support.

Finally, we thank the scores of young clergy with whom we have had the privilege of working in the last three years, those who participated in our survey, and those who shared their stories in other ways. Without their candor and openness, this book would not have been possible. They have renewed our hope in the future of the church and inspired us to communicate to the broader church both the challenges and opportunities they see in ministering to a new millennium.

The scholar James MacGregor Burns has said of American society, "One of the most universal cravings in our time is a hunger for compelling and creative leadership."[3] For the church to be adequate to its calling in our time, it must attend to the need to develop in each generation thoroughly qualified, compelling, and creative leadership. We must cultivate anew in rising generations the understanding that ordained ministry is a way of life, not simply a profession; that ministry is a calling, not a career. In contrast to a success culture and a maintenance church, we must hold up to today's young believers a model of leadership in service to God's great vision for the world.

Lovett H. Weems Jr.
Ann A. Michel

CHAPTER ONE

Dimensions of the Young Clergy Crisis

Young clergy are an endangered species.
Be very good to them.
Bishop Robert Schnase

At a recent pastors' school with several hundred clergy present, a bishop asked all the clergy under the age of 35 to stand. Four or five stood. The bishop said, "All the rest of you look very carefully at these young clergy persons. In our conference, they are an endangered species. Be very good to them."

In recent decades, many North American churches have suffered a serious and sustained decline in the number and percentage of clergy under the age of 35. In many denominations, the percentage of younger clergy has slipped close to 5 percent or even less. For some time, observers have feared that the numbers of younger clergy had declined. Anecdotal evidence, seminary enrollment trends, and the general perception of a graying clergy all gave rise to concern, but the magnitude of the trend had not been documented due to limited available data. Clergy ages are not easy to track because few church agencies maintain up-to-date age information on clergy.

In 2005 and 2006, the Lewis Center for Church Leadership of Wesley Theological Seminary set about the task of documenting clergy age trends. The work began with data from the General Board of Pension and Health Benefits of The United Methodist Church. The primary focus of the project was on United Methodist elders, but the Center also collected available data on clergy age trends in other denominations. The findings were issued in a March 2006 report, *Clergy Age Trends in The United Methodist Church: 1985–2005*. The research included elders, deacons, and local pastors, but the primary focus was on the increasing age of elders. Since then, the Center has updated the original research with data from 2006 and 2007.

This research revealed a situation even worse than many feared. The percentage of United Methodist elders age 35 and under has decreased from 15.05 percent in 1985 to 4.92 percent in 2007. And because the pool of elders is smaller today than it was in 1985, the drop off in actual numbers has been far greater than in percentages. In 1985, there were 3,219 elders under 35 out of a total of 21,378. In 2007, there were only 876 elders under 35 among The United Methodist Church's 17,800 elders.[1] Looking back further, the trend is even more pronounced. According to Division of Ordained Ministry estimates, in 1973, 21.2 percent of United Methodist clergy were under the age of 35.

What about Other Denominations?

Many other denominations participating in this research project reported similarly low numbers of clergy under 35. In 2007, the percentage of clergy under 35 in the American Baptist Church was 5.1 percent; in the Episcopal Church, it was 3.43 percent; and in the Evangelical Lutheran Church in America (ELCA), it was 5.92 percent. In 2006, the Christian Church

(Disciples of Christ) had 5.53 percent of clergy under 35, and the Presbyterian Church (USA) reported 6.2 percent.

Other denominations reporting low percentages of young clergy are the Seventh Day Adventist Church with only 1.19 percent of their clergy under 35, and the United Church of Canada reporting 2.66 percent. A 2001 survey of American Roman Catholic priests indicated that only 3.1 percent were under 35.

Some participating denominations that reported higher percentages of young clergy included the Assemblies of God at 7.16 percent (2006 figures), Church of God (Anderson, Indiana) at 8.41 percent, the Church of the Nazarene at 10.68 percent, and the Lutheran Church-Missouri Synod at 8.34 percent.[2]

Comparisons among denominations are not exact. Some denominations have more current figures than others, and educational requirements for ordination vary. Since pension programs provide the only source of consistently reliable age data, the percentage of clergy participating in pension plans can make a difference. Nevertheless, there is striking similarity in the low percentage of clergy under age 35 in a number of different denominations.

Clergy Age Comparisons Across Denominations

By Percentage			
Denomination	**Under 35**	**35 - 54**	**55 - 70**
American Baptist	5.10%	51.35%	43.54%
Assemblies of God *2006 Data*	7.16%	54.64%	38.20%
Christian Church (DOC) *2006 Data*	5.3%	50.92%	43.78%
Church of God (Anderson, Ind.)	8.41%	52.24%	39.34%
Church of the Nazarene	10.68%	54.00%	35.31%
Episcopal Church	3.43%	37.81%	58.76%
Evangelical Lutheran Church (ELCA)	5.92%	50.57%	43.50%

Lutheran Church (Missouri Synod)	8.34%	54.59%	37.07%
Presbyterian Church (USA)	6.20%	51.39%	42.41%
Roman Catholic (U.S.) 2001	3.10%	31.70%	65.20%
Seventh Day Adventist	1.19%	44.72%	54.09%
United Church of Canada	2.62%	49.56%	47.82%
United Methodist Church	4.92%	50.74%	44.34%

By Numbers			
Denomination	**Under 35**	**35 - 54**	**55 - 70**
American Baptist	247	2,486	2,108
Assemblies of God *2006 Data*	998	7,620	5,327
Christian Church (DOC) *2006 Data*	223	2,142	1,842
Church of God (Anderson, Ind.)	278	1,726	1,300
Church of the Nazarene	623	3,150	2,060
Episcopal Church	408	4,500	6,993
Evangelical Lutheran Church (ELCA)	659	5,625	4,839
Lutheran Church (Missouri Synod)	451	2,952	2,005
Presbyterian Church (USA)	594	4,921	4,061
Seventh Day Adventist	29	1,088	1,316
United Church of Canada	59	1,116	1,077
United Methodist Church	876	9,032	7,892

Aging Elders

With the decline in young elders has come an increase in the percentage of elders in the upper age brackets of the United Methodist Church. The proportion of elders who are 55 and older increased from 27 percent in 1985 to 44 percent in 2007. The average age of elders increased from 46.8 to 51.98, and the median age (half older, half younger) rose from 48 to 53. The single most represented age among United Methodist elders in 2006 and 2007 was 59—reflecting the age of those who were born in the first two years of the baby boom. The portion of elders over 55 is also above 40 percent in the American Baptist Church, Christian Church (Disciples of Christ), Episcopal Church, Evangelical Lutheran Church in America, Presbyterian Church (USA), Seventh Day Adventist Church, and the United Church of Canada.

Regional Variations

The decline in young clergy has not affected all regions equally. At 41 percent, the Southeastern Jurisdiction of the United Methodist Church has more young clergy than any of the other regional jurisdictions in the United States. The Arkansas Conference had the highest percentage of young clergy among its members in 2007, with 8.8 percent under 35. But this is still 7 percent below the average for the whole denomination in 1985. The Western North Carolina Conference had the largest number of young elders in 2007 with 55.

While the percentage and numerical declines vary, every jurisdiction and conference has suffered a significant decline in recent years. Out of 63 annual conferences, 26 conferences each (over 40 percent) had less than 10 elders who were under 35 in 2007. In 15 annual conferences, the number of young elders could be counted on the fingers of one hand.

Seminary Enrollment Trends

Data provided by the Association of Theological Schools in the United States and Canada (ATS) show that in 1995 about 39 percent of Master of Divinity degree students were under 30. By 2005 there was an increase in the percentage of young seminarians with about 42 percent under 30, but a majority were still older. The percentage of students under 30 attending United Methodist seminaries in 2005 was 37 percent or 5 percent below the ATS average. However, the percentage of students at United Methodist seminaries under 30 has increased every year since 1997 when the percentage had dipped to 29 percent. While some theological schools have significant or at least increasing numbers of young students, the number of young seminary students is but one factor in how many young clergy there will be in the future, particularly how many there will be serving in congregational ministry.

More and more seminary graduates—particularly younger graduates—are pursuing ministries other than traditional parish ministry. Research by the Center for the Study of Theological Education of Auburn Theological Seminary in New York City found that a higher percentage of older students planned to be ordained than younger seminarians. Moreover, younger students are more likely than their older classmates to be headed for campus ministry, mission, teaching, or graduate study.[3] A much-discussed story in the *New York Times* carried the title "Students Flock to Seminaries, but Fewer See Pulpit in Future."[4] The declining number of young elders seems to reflect this trend.

Is Attrition a Factor?

Attrition is a subject of much speculation. Many wonder if young clergy dropping out of ministry might be a factor in their low numbers. The Auburn research project is not able to answer these questions for specific age groups, but researcher Barbara G.

Wheeler was able to compare their overall data with United Methodist responses for this book project.

The overall finding on attrition among all denominations is that it tends to be about 1 percent a year for the first 10 years, a rate much lower than many had assumed and not significantly different from other professional school graduates. Wheeler reports that United Methodist attrition rates are slower in the first 5 years (2 percent leave ministry and 4 percent leave parish ministry, compared with 5 percent for both categories across all denominations). But she finds that United Methodist attrition tends to be about the same after 10 years (11 percent attrition from parish ministry) as other denominations. She does find that United Methodist women enter ministry and congregational ministry at only slightly lower rates than men, but their attrition rates are higher, especially from parish ministry.

An encouraging finding is that a high percentage of United Methodist clergy plan on staying in ministry, and a fairly high percentage plan to stay in parish ministry—higher percentages than the average for all clergy across denominations.[5] While these findings are based on United Methodist clergy of all ages, they correspond to what the Lewis Center found in its survey of young clergy. Almost all the respondents said they agreed with the statement, "I expect to be an active United Methodist clergy five years from now."

In additional research, though not differentiated by age, Auburn further explored details about those choosing or not choosing parish ministry after seminary. They discovered that the time of greatest attrition occurs upon seminary graduation in terms of those who choose not to enter congregational ministry, despite the fact that many more students enter parish ministry than say they intend to when they begin seminary. They have found that about half of those graduating from seminary with a Master of Divinity degree in 2000 were headed for congregational ministry when they entered seminary, but almost two-thirds of them say upon graduation that they intend to serve in a congregation and fully three-quarters end up serving in a congregation.[6]

Putting Clergy Age Trends in Perspective

Discussion of the declining number of young clergy often leads to questions: isn't this just a symptom of the aging of America? Don't all young people take longer to grow up and settle into professions these days? Aren't these trends just a reflection of declining church membership? Clergy age trends do need to be understood in terms of larger trends in American society and the church, but these broader trends cannot explain away the young clergy crisis. Comparing age statistics from the United Methodist Church with other demographic variables makes this point.

In comparing the number of young clergy to general population trends, 25- to 34-year-olds are the relevant comparison group. Since 25 is the age at which someone is likely to be commissioned if they go to seminary right after college, it is the bottom of the age range for young clergy.

The overall population between 25 and 34 has declined since 1985—from about 42 million to about 40 million—despite an overall increase in the U.S. population. However, the decline in young elders has been much greater. Between 1985 and 2005, the ratio of young elders to the total population of 25- to 34-year-olds fell from one-to-13,000 to one for every 47,000. In other words, the ratio of young clergy to the general population of their age is more than 3 times less than it was 20 years ago.

Can the decline in young clergy be explained in terms of broader social trends—younger people living at home longer, marrying later, and taking longer to finish school? Some sociological data and considerable anecdotal evidence seem to point to such trends, at least in some segments of the population. But if the decline in young clergy were merely a function of these broader social phenomena, it would stand to reason that the number of young persons in other professions would also be declining dramatically. Looking at dentistry—for example, a profession that requires about the same amount of schooling as ordained ministry—one finds that approximately 14 percent of dentists but less than 5 percent of clergy, in most mainline denominations, are under 35.[7] Additionally, the mean age of beginning seminary students is considerably higher than what is found in other graduate-level professional education, such as law and medicine.[8]

Clergy age trends also relate, of course, to other church demographic trends. The total church membership in the United Methodist Church declined between 1985 and 2005, as did the total number of elders, the number of churches, and the number of pastoral charges. But the decline in the number of young clergy has been proportionally much greater than any of these other changes. Total membership, for example, fell from 9,154,364 to 7,995,429. However, the ratio of young elders to members also declined—from one young elder for every 2,900 members to one for every 9,127 members.

The total number of elders also decreased between 1985 and 2007, from 21,378 to 17,800. Unfortunately, however, the drop in young elders has been proportionally larger. The percentage of young elders declined from 15.06 percent to 4.92 percent of the total. In 1985, one of every 7 elders was under 35. In 2007, only one elder in 20 was under 35. To put it another way, from 1985 to 2007, the total decline in the number of elders was 3,578. The decline in the under-35 age bracket was 2,343, or 73 percent of the total.

Ratios of Young Clergy to Other Variables

	1985	2005
Ratio of young elders to U.S. population of 25 to 34-year-olds	1:13,000	1:47,000
Ratio of young elders to church membership	1:2,900	1:9,500
Ratio of young elders to total number of elders	1:7	1:20
Ratio of young elders to churches	1:12	1:41
Ratio of young elders to pastoral charges	1:8	1:31

Likewise, the decline in young elders has been significantly greater than the decrease in the number of churches and pastoral charges. In 1985, the denomination had one young elder for every 12 churches. By 2005, this had declined to one for every 41 churches. The ratio of young elders to pastoral charges decreased from one-to-8 to one-to-31.

Anyone dismissing concerns about the drop in young clergy because of the general decline of the denomination would be missing the point. That kind of logic would ultimately lead to a situation where no young clergy are needed because there are no longer congregations to serve. The best way to ensure that day never comes is to replenish the supply of young clergy.

CHAPTER TWO

A Profile of Today's Young Clergy

Many of the people insist that they can't understand how [someone] so young as I could possibly be a preacher. Since I am twenty-three their reaction to my youth simply means that they find something incompatible even between the ripe age of twenty-three and the kind of seasoned wisdom which they expect from the pulpit.[1]
Reinhold Niebuhr

What can be said about young clergy today? Statistical data from the General Board of Pension and Health Benefits (GBOPHB) and results from the Lewis Center's 2007 survey of young United Methodist clergy provide a demographic portrait of young clergy today, including what characterizes them and where they are serving.

In 2007, there are 876 elders (commissioned and ordained) under the age of 35 in the United Methodist Church. This represents 4.92 percent of active elders. There are currently 64 deacons (commissioned and ordained) under 35, representing 7.1 percent of all active deacons who are part of the denominational pension plan. And there are 376 under-35 local pastors, representing 5.48 percent of all active local pastors. The total for young local pastors includes both full and part-time but not student local pastors. It is surprising, perhaps, that a higher percentage of persons under 35 are local pastors than elders, since local pastors have traditionally had an older age profile. (The older age at which local pastors entered was often given as a reason that the Course of Study educational route was more realistic for them than a seminary degree program.)

The statistics from GBOPHB regarding deacons may not give an accurate picture of all deacons presently serving in the denomination. A large percentage of deacons have pension programs through agencies other than the United Methodist program because of their places of primary employment. The same is true for some elders and local pastors, but, compared to deacons, a much smaller percentage of elders and local pastors do not have an account with the GBOPHB.

Clergy Under 35 as a Percentage of Overall Clergy

2007	Number	Percent
Elders under 35 (commissioned and ordained)	876	4.92
Deacons under 35 (commissioned and ordained)	64	7.10
Local pastors under 35	376	5.48

Gender

The GBHOPB statistics reveal that 67 percent of these young elders are men and 33 percent are women. Forty percent of the young elders responding to the Lewis Center's survey were women. The percentage of women among young elders, at 33 percent, is higher than it is in other age categories; women are 25.8 percent of elders age 35 to 54, and 24.1 percent of those over 55. But the gain in the percentage of women is not as high as some might expect among this youngest generation, given changing gender-role expectations and the sizable number of women in seminaries. It seems that men still account for the vast majority of elders whose first career is ministry. The gender breakdown among young deacons is just the opposite from young elders, with 62.5 percent women and 37.5 percent men. Seventy-six percent of young local pastors are men; 23.94 percent are women.

Marital Status

The vast majority of young clergy who responded to the Lewis Center survey are married—78 percent of elders, 73 percent of local pastors, and 53 percent of deacons. In this sense, they are markedly different from their peers in the general population. The *New York Times* recently reported that married couples, whose numbers have been declining for decades as a proportion of American households, have finally slipped into a minority, and among those aged 25 to 34, they have been in the minority for more than five years.[2] The *Times* article quotes a Brookings Institution demographer, William H. Frey, who says, "This would seem to close the book on the Ozzie and Harriet era that characterized much of the last century."[3] One wonders why young clergy are so much more likely to be married than their age peers in the general population and what this disparity means for their ability to connect with their peers. There is this sharp disparity among young clergy (22 percent single) amidst a generation, where single lifestyles are increasingly common—more than 50 percent in this age group.

Male young clergy are more likely to be married than their female colleagues. Among young male elders, 88 percent are married compared to only 63 percent of the female young elders. To put it another way: among young elders who are single, the percentage of women is almost twice that of men—64 percent compared to only 36 percent. The fact that the percentage of married deacons is low in comparison to elders is consistent with the fact that young female clergy are more likely to be unmarried, and almost two-thirds of young deacons are female.

Race

The GBOPHB does not keep statistics on race, but the Lewis Center's survey provides some data on the racial breakdown of young clergy. Of the young elders responding to the Lewis Center survey, just under 96 percent were white, with the remaining 4 percent coming from African American, Asian/Pacific Islanders, Hispanic/Latino/Latina, Native American, and Multiracial. Young deacons and local pastors are somewhat more diverse, with whites accounting for 86 percent and 85 percent respectively.

It must be noted that these percentages are based on those young clergy completing the survey. While the response rate to the survey was exceptionally high (about half of the young elders), there is no way to verify that these racial breakdowns match the total young clergy population. If the survey respondents are roughly representative, the percentage of young clergy in different racial/ethnic categories is less than the percentage of these groups in the broader church. It should also be noted that denominational percentages can be misleading, since there is significant regional variation in the percentage of racial/ethnic clergy.

Distribution of Young Elders by Jurisdictions and Conferences

The distribution of young elders is not proportionate among the conferences and jurisdictions that make up the United Methodist Church in the United States. Of all the young elders, 42 percent are found in just one of the five jurisdictions—the Southeastern Jurisdiction. The South Central and North Central Jurisdictions each have 19 percent of the young elders. The Northeastern Jurisdiction has 13 percent, and the Western Jurisdiction has just 7 percent.

The conferences with the highest percentages and largest numbers of young elders in 2007 are as follows:

Top Ten Conferences for Young Elders—2007

By Percentage		**By Number**	
Arkansas	8.80%	Western North Carolina	53
Holston *	8.70%	North Georgia	38
Oklahoma	8.51%	Virginia	36
North Alabama	8.42%	Florida	32
Dakotas	8.28%	North Alabama	31
Alabama-West Florida	8.19%	South Carolina	29
Western North Carolina	7.59%	Holston *	28
Mississippi	7.14%	Oklahoma	28
North Carolina	7.14%	Mississippi	26
Central Texas	6.91%	North Carolina	26

* The Holston Conference includes parts of southwestern Virginia, east Tennessee, and north Georgia.

Type of Appointment

According to the Lewis Center survey, 49 percent of young elders are senior or solo pastors; 39 percent are associates; 5 percent are in campus ministry. Most of the young associates are found in two jurisdictions—Southeastern and South Central. Together, these two jurisdictions account for 70 percent of the young clergy *associate* positions. Looking at it another way, 45 percent of the young elders in the Southeastern Jurisdiction serve as associates, 44 percent in the South Central Jurisdiction, 34 percent in the North Central Jurisdiction, and only 15 percent in the Northeastern Jurisdiction. Although the percentage of associates among those responding to the survey from the Western Jurisdiction was the highest—54 percent—this jurisdiction accounted for only 7 percent of the young elders in the survey.

There are fewest associates in the Western and Northeastern Jurisdictions where there are fewer large membership churches.

The survey reported that 80 percent of young elders serve one congregation; 15 percent serve two-point charges; and 4 percent serve charges with three or more churches. Ninety-three percent of young elders are serving full time, compared to 83 percent of young deacons and only 45 percent of young local pastors who responded to the Lewis Center survey. Thirty-three percent of young elders serve in towns, 28 percent in suburbs, 22 percent in rural areas, and 17 percent in urban areas.

Thirty-five percent of young elders are serving in their first year in their current appointment, 25 percent in their second year, and 19 percent in their third. Almost 11 percent are serving in their fourth year, and about 10 percent have been at their current appointment for five or more years.

Size of Church

The survey indicates that 39 percent of young elders serve small congregations with average worship attendance of 100 or less, and 24 percent serve congregations with average attendance between 100 and 250. While 20 percent serve congregations with an average of 251 to 500 in attendance at worship, 17 percent are in congregations with average worship attendance of 500 or more.

However, in separating young associates from those in senior or solo pastor roles, one finds that all of the young elders serving congregations with more than 500 in worship are in associate roles. Among young elders who are solo or senior pastors, 67 percent serve congregations with less than 100 in worship, and only 3 percent are in churches with average attendance greater than 250.

Satisfaction in Ministry

By and large, the 25- to 34-year-olds who have chosen the path of ordained ministry are satisfied with their work, their ministry settings, their support networks, and their life circumstances. Responses to a variety of questions in the Lewis Center's survey indicate a high level of satisfaction in ministry. For example, 94 percent feel they are growing in effectiveness in ministry; 86 percent say those they serve would say their current appointment is a good fit; and almost 70 percent say their current appointment is appropriate to their spiritual gifts. Of those who are married, 91 percent say their spouse is supportive of their ministry; 85 percent are connected with supportive friends and colleagues beyond their families; and 80 percent feel supported by those they serve. Less than 4 percent did not expect to remain in ministry over the next five years. And 77 percent would recommend ordained ministry in The United Methodist Church to other young persons. Moreover, the majority of young elders feel that their congregations are growing spiritually, numerically, and missionally and are positive about the future of the denomination.

These levels of satisfaction are strikingly high. And it is particularly noteworthy that satisfaction levels remain high when different segments of the young elder population are examined. Male and female, married and single, associate and solo pastors all register high levels of satisfaction, as do those serving in all different kinds of communities, and even those in the lowest salary brackets. Within this pattern of consistently high rankings, however, one slight deviation should be noted. Young clergy who are single are the only group whose satisfaction indicators, when they deviate from the average, are consistently lower. Single young clergy seem to be slightly less comfortable in their ministry settings than others. One question asked singles about their social connections, and 46 percent disagreed with the statement, "I am able to date or pursue social connections."

Young Elders' Levels of Satisfaction

Percentage of young elders who agree strongly or very strongly with each statement	
I feel I am growing in my effectiveness as a pastoral leader.	94%
My spouse is supportive of my ministry.	91%
Those in my appointment would say it is "a good fit."	86%
I stay connected with supportive friends and colleagues outside of family.	85%
I expect to be an active United Methodist clergy five years from now.	84%
My current appointment is helping me develop as an effective pastor.	82%
I feel supported by those I serve in my appointment.	80%
I am likely to recommend ordained ministry in the UMC to other young people.	77%
My current appointment is appropriate based on my spiritual gifts.	69%

What can be said of these findings? At one level, they are surprising given the common perception that many young clergy are beleaguered, dissatisfied, and on the verge of dropping out of ministry. However, these findings do not mean that young clergy have no problems or concerns. Much of the remainder of this book is devoted to issues and concerns related to the status and well-being of young clergy. Research shows that a certain segment of the young clergy population is struggling financially, that a growing percentage has significant educational debts, and that many experience generational tensions as they minister in an aging church. It is encouraging, however, that despite these pressures, young clergy are on the whole optimistic and dedicated to their calling.

It is helpful to keep in mind that high levels of career satisfaction are the norm among American clergy. A report released in 2007 by the National Opinion Research Center at the University of Chicago found that 87 percent of clergy are satisfied in their

Young Elders' Levels of Satisfaction By Category

	All	Male	Female	Single	Solo/Senoir	Assoc	Rural	Urban	Town	Suburban	Salary<$30,000
I feel I am growing in my effectiveness as a pastoral leader.	94%	93%	95%	94%	96%	91%	97%	95%	96%	94%	93%
My spouse is supportive of my ministry.	91%	90%	92%		93%	90%	90%	90%	90%	91%	90%
Those in my appointment would say it is "a good fit."	86%	85%	87%	73%	85%	83%	81%	82%	85%	87%	78%
I stay connected with supportive friends and colleagues outside of family.	85%	83%	87%	83%	80%	86%	87%	85%	81%	82%	82%
I expect to be an active United Methodist clergy five years from now.	84%	87%	81%	84%	83%	82%	88%	89%	78%	79%	84%
My current appointment is helping me develop as an effective pastor.	82%	81%	83%	77%	86%	78%	83%	82%	83%	80%	80%
I feel supported by those I serve in my appointment.	80%	82%	79%	75%	80%	78%	83%	76%	78%	81%	89%
I am likely to recommend ordained ministry in the UMC to other young people.	77%	79%	74%	70%	75%	78%	79%	73%	71%	76%	70%
My current appointment is appropriate based on my spiritual gifts.	69%	71%	66%	67%	69%	68%	67%	68%	69%	70%	67%

jobs. In fact, clergy topped the list of all other occupations in terms of job satisfaction and general happiness.[4] So in this sense, young clergy are representative of their older colleagues.

Finally, these findings are helpful in clarifying the causes of the young clergy shortage. There is a common misperception that the decline in the number of young elders is the result of their "dropping out of ministry in droves." Data on attrition rates do not support that hypothesis. The high levels of satisfaction in ministry reflected in these survey findings reinforce our conclusion that the decline in young clergy is caused more by fewer young people entering the profession than it is by the number who drop out after having responded to a call.

Perhaps the most important conclusion that can be drawn from this overall demographic portrait is that, in many ways, young clergy reflect the dynamics of the larger church in which they serve. More in this generation are female, but, like clergy in the church at large, most are still male. Most young elders are in the South, where, by many measures, United Methodist churches tend to be stronger. Most young elders serve in smaller congregations, and most United Methodist congregations are small. And like other clergy, most find satisfaction in ministry.

CHAPTER THREE

Why Young Clergy Matter

Young clergy aren't necessarily better. They're just younger. And that matters.
Lovett H. Weems Jr.

A fundamental assumption of this inquiry must be stated unequivocally: God calls people of all ages to ministry. The problem is not an overabundance of persons over 35 engaged in or discerning a call to ministry. Rather, the dilemma is that the church is allowing so many younger persons to ignore God's call. Nothing in this analysis is intended to diminish the vital contributions of middle-aged and older pastors, including second-career pastors, who often bring to the position important life skills and church experience as they enter ministry. Persons of all ages bring vital gifts to the practice of ministry, and it will continue to be crucial for the church to offer to each one the tools for discerning God's call and the support to respond.

There are also a number of important reasons why the pool of clergy must include a proportionate number of younger persons. The declining number of young clergy deprives the profession at both ends of the age spectrum. The new ideas, creativity, energy, and cultural awareness often exhibited by the young are lost. With more persons entering ministry with fewer years to serve, the wisdom and experience that can come with long tenures in ministry are also in jeopardy.

The Constitution of the United States affords 25-year-olds the right to serve in the United States House of Representatives. At 21, a physician can be licensed to practice medicine in the state of New York.[1] Yet 28 is generally the youngest age at which one can be ordained elder in The United Methodist Church; and those who are elders in their 20s or early 30s often are thought not to be ready for particularly challenging assignments. This is despite the fact that younger clergy have illustrated that they are capable of great things: Martin Luther King Jr. was 26 when he led the Montgomery Bus Boycott, and John Wesley was in his mid-30s as the Wesleyan Revival began.

Church leaders who gathered recently to discuss clergy age trends were asked the question: "Why are young clergy important?" They responded with comments such as, "Younger clergy have an ability to see the world and the church through new eyes," "They bring enthusiasm, idealism, and fresh perspectives to the practice of ministry," and "Young clergy are more open to innovation and more nimble in working with new ideas."

In many instances, young clergy bring tremendous energy to the demands of ministry because of the mental and physical stamina associated with youth. The schedules and routines of the young may be more flexible, and as well, they are available for and interested in innovative challenges holding significant risk. To put it in common vernacular, older people tend to be more set in their ways.

The Lewis Center for Church Leadership is in the early stages of a research project on clergy pastoral effectiveness. Some initial findings, which will need to be subjected to much broader testing, indicate that as clergy get older, they tend to rate themselves somewhat high in their leadership effectiveness. However, laity responses do not follow that pattern. Laity tend to rate younger clergy as high, and often higher, than they rate either clergy ages 35–54 or ages 55–70. In all cases, the differences across age cohorts are not great, indicating perhaps that while clergy may tend to gain self-confidence as they acquire more experience, the laity perception of clergy effectiveness is quite positive for younger, less experienced clergy.

Young clergy have certain advantages in reaching out to their own generation. They are more likely to speak the language of an emerging generation whose worldview and communication modes differ from those of their parents' generation. They show high sensitivity to diversity and other cultural realities in today's world. Just as important, the mere presence of young clergy in a church symbolizes that younger persons are valued as leaders and participants. A young pastor from Maryland believes that many young families have chosen her church because they see her and other young adults in leadership roles. Although creative and vibrant older pastors can also connect with younger generations, "Young people can feel intimidated by a church where the same leaders have served for decades," she says.

"You need young clergy to model for other young people that you can have young people in the church," says a 30-something pastor from Wisconsin. "Being younger does help in connecting with younger generations. In the small church I'm serving, membership has gone up by 50 percent. There are so many more people in their 20s and 30s because they look at me as somebody to whom they can relate—someone who knows what it's like to be a young adult today." Diversity of every kind is helpful in pulpits, including age diversity, because, whether we like it or not, people often seek out congregations where there are people with whom they can identify. "Commonalities make people feel connected," says one young pastor. "Young persons often feel they do not belong in congregations where there is a sea of gray-haired people and all the clergy and leaders are older." Younger clergy are also a model to youth in the church, especially those who might be experiencing a call to ministry. "It's important for a 16- or 17-year-old about to go to college and thinking about seminary to see young pastors who have walked that same walk. In any profession, it's important for those entering to see that those ahead of them have a story that is kind of like their own," says a younger pastor from Kansas.

All of these factors help explain why young clergy seem particularly well-suited to the task of church planting. Research conducted in the Episcopal Church has found that pastors between the ages of 24 and 35 were the most successful in founding churches that reached 250 or more in worship attendance within seven years.[2] When conference staff persons responsible for new church starts in The United Methodist Church gathered at a recent national event, they were asked, "If you were starting a church in your conference, what age pastor would you prefer?" When the group shared the preferred ages they had individually selected, the range was between 25 and 35. One of the largest and most influential United Methodist churches today, The United Methodist Church of the Resurrection in Kansas, was started by Adam Hamilton, who was 25 when appointed (and, as he likes to say, "looked 15").

Research on the differences between younger and older seminary students sheds light on some other attributes of younger clergy. Younger and older students tend to enter seminary with different gifts. Not surprisingly, younger students are more likely to have been involved in church youth organizations and campus ministry; whereas older students are more likely to have had a deep involvement with a local congregation.[3] Younger students tend to enter seminary with better academic records in college or previous graduate studies, including significantly higher grade-point averages and more academic or nonacademic awards in college. They are also more likely to have educational training in disciplines such as theology, religion, philosophy, and other humanities traditionally regarded as appropriate preparation for theological study.[4]

Just as youthfulness has advantages in ministry, so does experience. Leadership is a form of expertise that has a long gestation period. In *Building Leaders*, Jay Conger and Beth Benjamin explain that in most fields, attaining the status of expert requires at least ten years of extensive experience and training.[5] Moreover, there is evidence in secular career development studies that the period from age 30 to 40 is critical in determining long-term success. In *Young Clergy: A Biographical-Developmental Study*, Donald Capps tested the extent to which this theory applies to ministry by examining the biographies of some of history's most influential ministers. He concluded that the middle to late 30s were the most decisive years in determining success in ministry. Growth and progress in these years is what lays a solid foundation for the next 25 years of ministry.[6] These studies reinforce a conclusion attested to by simple common sense—expertise and success in ministry come with long-term career growth and development. Persons who enter ministry at a young age can devote a lifetime to serving the church and honing their ministry skills.

Without sufficient numbers of younger persons entering the profession, there will be fewer clergy in the pipeline who have achieved the longevity of service required for the most challenging pastoral assignments and denominational leadership roles. The growing numbers of middle-aged and older persons who enter ministry bring many important gifts; it is also true that many will not achieve the longevity of service needed for some of the most demanding ministry roles. Many of these positions, such as serving as lead pastor of a very large congregation, require not only 10 to 15 years of experience, but also 10 to 15 years left to serve—for it hardly seems wise to appoint someone on the brink of retirement to a significant ministry that will take many years to develop fully. Factoring this into the equation, it becomes readily apparent how critical it is to have a steady stream of younger clergy entering ministry.

A middle-aged clergyman from Texas makes this argument quite eloquently:

> In my conference there are 35 churches that averaged 700 or more in their weekly worship services. All of these congregations need pastors gifted in preaching ability, leadership, and administrative skills (including staffing). Whereas the number of these congregations has increased almost fivefold over the past generation, our pastoral leadership resources have not

> increased at the same rate. While many of our second-career pastors are very bright and gifted, they do not have the years left on the clock to gain the experience necessary to serve larger congregations well. By the time the most gifted of the second-career pastors gain the years of experience in multiple appointments that they need to be fully ready for a large church assignment, it is about time to retire. Younger persons have the time available to gain the experience necessary for these appointments. Unfortunately, there are fewer and fewer of them coming down the pike.

The dearth of young clergy is contributing to an impending leadership crisis in yet another way. The growing percentage of elders who are 55 and older raises the specter of a tidal wave of retirements hitting the system in the not-too-distant future. In 2007, over 44 percent of United Methodist elders were in the 55 to 70 age bracket, up from 27 percent in 1985. However, in some conferences more than half of the elders are over 55. United Methodist clergy may serve until they reach the age of 70, the mandatory retirement age; the trend, however, is toward earlier retirements. Since 2000, the average retirement age for United Methodist elders has been in a range between 63 and 65. Averaging the statistics for the past seven years reveals that elders tend to retire before reaching the age of 64.[7] As a result, in some areas, there will soon not be enough clergy to serve the congregations awaiting appointments.

The aging of the church's clergy pool poses a number of practical and institutional challenges, as well. There is widespread concern among pension and health care administrators in many denominations about the costs associated with having so many middle-aged and older persons in the system—costs for which, in some of our traditions, the whole church shares responsibility. The fact that younger people tend to be healthier is one of the factors that many of the administrators mentioned when asked why young clergy matter. They foresee less money flowing into pension trusts at the same time that more is being paid out, and they anticipate dramatic growth in pension and health costs as there are more older persons, who also may be less healthy, in benefit plans without the stability of younger, healthier participants paying premiums.[8] The church has always depended upon a wide range of age groups to keep the benefit programs in balance, and that balance can no longer be assumed.

Having a proportionate number of young persons entering ordained ministry is vital to the vibrancy of the church, as well as its ability to attract younger congregants and form new congregations. It is essential for developing the long-term experience in ministry necessary for the most challenging assignments. It is also necessary to ensure that there will be a sufficient number of elders in the coming decades. Young clergy do, indeed, matter.

CHAPTER FOUR

The Need for Enlistment

The achievement and maintenance of a strong and sufficient ministry is the responsibility, not of a board or an agency or a school, but of the whole Church. In the end our ministry will be as numerous or as scarce, as educated or as ignorant, as strong or as weak, as good or as bad as we as a church enable it to be.

William R. Cannon, speaking at the 1956 Methodist General Conference

It is easy for United Methodists to take for granted the presence of an educated clergy. This has not always been the case. A college may have been established at the Christmas Conference in 1784, but it took fifty years before a theological school was begun. Then it took generations of faithful lay and clergy leaders to develop what is arguably the finest denominational family of seminaries in the United States.

Today the church faces a new challenge. As our need for more compelling and creative leadership grows, our church is seeing fewer persons enter ordained ministry—especially fewer young persons. The church is also in danger of not having the quality of leadership it requires. God is always calling persons to ministry. However, all of us in the church are recognizing in a new way the need to work together to encourage and support persons in hearing and responding to this call.

A Common Calling

The responsibility for identification and enlistment for ordained ministry is shared by many in the United Methodist Church. Laity in congregations, pastors and deacons, bishops and district superintendents, boards of ordained ministry and seminaries are some who share a common calling to encourage and guide those who seek to serve God in this way.

When things are not going well, different segments within organizations tend to blame each other. In the church, for example, local churches and conferences may say, "The seminaries just don't send us good enough graduates." And seminary faculty may say, "The churches don't send us good enough students." In United Methodist polity, however, the historic power to determine fitness for ministry has been given to the annual conferences. So when it comes to the enlistment, quality, preparation, and standards of ordained ministry, we have an issue together—a common calling.

We are all partners in this great task. While each has particular roles and assignments, we cannot achieve what is needed by the church without working together. These are indeed good days to talk about collaborative efforts because of the openness of denominational, local church, and seminary leaders to cooperation around enlistment for ministry, as well as other major issues facing our denomination.

Some Trends

God calls all kinds of persons to the ministry—persons of all ethnicities and socioeconomic backgrounds, men and women, young and old, and persons from different countries throughout the world. Part of the work of enlistment is to ensure that none of the people God calls is overlooked, excluded, or allowed to ignore God's call. In recent years, those enrolling in North American seminaries have included more female students, racial/ethnic students, international students, and older students. This diversification is welcome and encouraging. Unfortunately, however, many younger persons are being allowed to ignore God's call.

Increasing diversity in professional education is not unique to the religious sector. Over the past generation, for example, an increasing proportion of women are entering the secular professions as well as ordained ministry. Medical and law schools have shown increases higher than theological schools. The enrollment of women in United Methodist seminaries in the United States is significantly higher than in theological schools as a whole because some denominations do not permit the ordination of women. Currently, women make up just over half of the students at United Methodist seminaries seeking the Master of Divinity degree that leads to ordination.

Today about one-third of the students at United Methodist seminaries are racial/ethnic students.[1] The need for such diversity is highlighted by the fact that the increasing racial/ethnic diversity of the United States will be a major demographic trend for years to come. In addition, there is a greater presence on seminary campuses of students from outside the United States and from numerous language and cultural backgrounds. This growth is fueled in part by the rapid growth of immigrant congregations in the United States and their needs for indigenous, trained leadership. It also springs from the efforts of seminaries to respond to the needs of an increasingly global church.

Seminaries also have seen an increase in students who have delayed vocational decisions or graduate study for a few years after college, and in students over 30 who are often referred to as *second-career* students, though this term does not precisely fit all of them. While the younger students bring immediate academic experience, the older seminarians bring rich life experience and normally have had extensive leadership experience in the local church. Each learns from the other and shares a deep appreciation for the gifts of one another.

Efforts to Enlist Young Candidates for Ministry

The increasing average age of United Methodist clergy and the declining numbers of young seminarians has led to renewed denominational efforts to lift up the call to full-time ministry for the young. One of the early enlistment projects funded by the Lilly Endowment, Inc., was sponsored by the Division of Ordained Ministry and the United Methodist seminaries. This was an important first step for the denomination in reclaiming the task of the enlistment of youth. In 1990, this project made possible "Exploration," the first national enlistment event in a decade for young people interested in ordained ministry. Planners hoped for at least 500 participants. Eventually registrations had to be cut off when they exceeded 1,000 because the budget and facilities could not handle more people. The overwhelming response to the first national Exploration event illustrates the importance of reaching out to younger persons. Exploration is now held every two years, and these subsequent events have been just as successful.

Young people who attended those early Exploration events are now among the finest young clergy leaders in the denomination. The Lewis Center survey shows that over 50 percent of young clergy participated as youth or college students in events such as that first one, in 1990, which intended to encourage them to enter ministry.

A pastor who served on the design team for the first Exploration event, after seeing so many excited young people there, wondered if there might be such youth in his own local church. When he went back home, he went separately to two youth leaders in his church and asked them if they had ever thought about ordained ministry. To his surprise, each of them said, "Yes, I have." This pastor asked himself, "How many other young people like these two have there been in my churches over the past thirty years, who needed me to encourage them?"

The Fund for Theological Education (FTE) currently is focusing on helping congregations identify and call forth young people from their midst whom God may be calling to ordained ministry. FTE staff member Elizabeth Mitchell Clement says they have found that congregations that send people into ordained ministry tend to do three things—notice, name, and nurture. Paying attention to young leaders in the congregation, helping them hear God's call by naming the gifts they see in the youth, and then nurturing them in the congregation and beyond, is a supportive and empowering approach.

FTE has identified and profiled several congregations whose habits and practices have proved effective in cultivating the next generation of pastoral leaders. Their research indicates that a congregation's commitment to nurture calling can be expressed in many different ways, indeed, each of the churches FTE studied has its own unique ways of nurturing call that flows naturally from their congregational identity and mission. Nevertheless, some important best practices for cultivating call can be extracted from these congregational profiles.[2]

The encouragement of young persons in ministry usually comes as part of a broad culture of call that provides opportunities for congregants of all ages to consider how God might be calling them to Christian service of all kinds. In such churches, the language of calling, Christian vocation, and summons to Christian service saturates congregational discourse and creates an atmosphere of invitation. From the pulpit and in other venues, this kind of congregation regularly lifts up as role models various persons who are active in ministry, encourages church members to reflect on their own call to service, and is intentional about delivering regular invitations for persons to consider ordained ministry.

A commitment to intergenerational ministry is another key ingredient. Providing opportunities for young persons to minister alongside more mature servants is important, as is a willingness to guide and mentor young persons actively. In the Lewis Center's

2007 survey, 88 percent of young United Methodist elders reported that at least one adult in the church had taken them seriously when they were youth. This factor, along with being involved in church as children at 88 percent, was the most common variable marking the path of today's young clergy into ministry. What is needed is "one-on-one work," said one respondent in an informal poll of denominational officials. "We need to learn not only how to relate to young people, but how to allow them to mentor us. We need to talk with them about what they see, what they question, what ideas they have."

It is most typical for young elders to have first considered entering ordained ministry before going to college (46 percent), to have received their call in the environment of their home congregation (44 percent), and to have experienced support from their pastor (85 percent). The factors most important to young elders in discerning their call were the desire to make a difference in the life of the church, the desire to serve others, the encouragement of clergy, their experience in a congregation, and their intellectual interest in religious and theological questions. These five factors were rated as important or very important by 75 percent or more of young elders. Factors that tended to be less important for most of these young clergy were major life events (such as death or divorce), campus ministry, and counseling and spiritual direction.

Perhaps we would all do well to remember the words of a seminary president who said, in 1905, that the principal reason why young people "of the highest qualifications are not entering the ministry in larger numbers is the lack of definite, earnest, prayerful efforts to influence them to devote themselves to this calling."[3]

Enlistment—Important but Not Sufficient

While thoughts turn immediately to enlistment when clergy shortages are discussed, we need to remember, as one young pastor put it, "Enlistment is only the beginning of the solution."

Enlistment may help with the yield—helping those already in the church respond to a call they are hearing. But it does not address the critical capacity issue: where are there signs of a vital and transformed church reaching out to active young people who are searching for new life in Christ? Enlistment must be done well and constantly, but, by itself, it will not be adequate to the task facing the church. In some ways, the situation is comparable to a congregation putting up signs, placing ads, and hosting events for newcomers in the community. All of these can help a church grow, but if the church itself is not vital and alive, no outreach efforts will finally be successful.

Nevertheless, there is no more important task before Christians today than the enlistment and education of leaders for the church. The future of the church depends upon such enlistment. In the coming years, a high percentage of current United Methodist pastors must be replaced. Even more important than the numbers is the church's need for clergy with outstanding gifts to meet the challenges of today and tomorrow. We must make no mistake about what is before us: what happens today in enlistment efforts will affect the church for decades to come.

There is no greater opportunity and responsibility than to be as involved as we all can be in the enlistment, encouragement, education, guidance, and approval of persons seeking to give their lives to God through ordained ministry.

CHAPTER FIVE

The Importance of Youth Ministry

Without a strong emphasis on caring for and nurturing young disciples, how can the Church expect young people to sense and follow calls to ministry? . . . If we want to see the Samuels, Timothys, Isaiahs, Jeremiahs, and Ruths of Gen Y and those following them, we better take time to re-evaluate our youth ministry.[1]
Erika Gara, young clergy pastor and blogger

The years prior to college are critical in shaping younger candidates for ministry. Campus ministries are also vitally important, but evidence suggests that youth ministry is most significant. Because local congregations play the primary role in sustaining ministry with young persons, efforts to increase the number of young clergy must revitalize congregational youth ministry, increase the number of youth involved, and reinforce congregational efforts to encourage young persons in their faith journeys.

According to the 2007 survey by the Lewis Center, 88 percent of the young United Methodist elders who responded were involved in church as children. Involvement in church during the high school years followed very closely behind, with over 87 percent of young elders involved in church during this stage of life. Somewhat fewer were active in faith connections during their college years, although the percentages are still sizable. Of today's young clergy, 65 percent were involved in a congregation during college, and 61 percent were involved in campus ministry.

Younger clergy most typically considered entering ordained ministry before going to college and received their call in a congregational environment. Among the young elders in the Lewis Center survey, 49 percent first considered entering ordained ministry before going to college, and 45 percent received their call in their home churches, with pastors topping the list of those who supported them in pursuing their call. Fourteen percent received their call in a congregation other than their home church, and 11 percent in camping ministries. Overall, 43 percent named the experience of a congregation as very important in discerning their call, while less than 2 percent said it had no importance in discerning their call.

In comparison, 36 percent were in college when they first considered entering ministry, and 19 percent said they received their call in the context of campus ministry. Twenty-two percent rated the experience of campus ministry as very important in discerning their call, but almost twice as many (39 percent) said campus ministry had no importance in discerning their call.

These findings are consistent with earlier research indicating that youth who are likely to enter seminary are those who participate in religious activities in high school and college.[2] The researchers also found that even among those who postpone entering a profession, the last two years of high school and the early years of college are an important time for making lasting career decisions. A survey of first-year seminarians in 1992 and 1993 found that two-thirds of the men and almost half of the women had first considered a religious profession in their high school or college years.[3]

The decline in the number of young clergy must, therefore, be considered in light of the declining number of youth and young persons active in local congregations. The pool from which young candidates for the ordained ministry are most likely to emerge is simply smaller. As one observer put it, "I think the young clergy crisis stems from the fact that we have so many dying churches. There are fewer active churches with active youth." According to Graham Reside of Vanderbilt Divinity School, "Some communities of faith have stopped thinking creatively about how to attract youth."[4]

Analyzing data on youth church school enrollment in United Methodist churches is one way to gauge trends. In 1985, youth between the ages of 14 and 18 who were enrolled in church school constituted 6.2 percent of the membership of United Methodist congregations; by 2005, this age group accounted for only 4.8 percent of members. Since total membership in the denomination also decreased significantly during this period, the drop in the absolute number of youth is more significant than the percentage decline. The number of high school youth decreased from 571,794 to 380,476—a drop of 33.6 percent with the rate of decline having increased significantly since 2000.

Not only are there fewer youth in churches today (using church school enrollment for comparison purposes), but a smaller percent of those who remain seem to be responding to God's call to ordained ministry. The ratio of young clergy to youth has declined significantly in recent decades, from one young elder per every 178 high-school-aged youth in 1985 to one per 447 youth in 2005.

Young Clergy and Youth

Year	UM Youth	UM Young Elders	Ratio of Young Elders to Youth
1985	571,794	3,219	1 to 178
1990	502,349	2,385	1 to 210
1995	522,971	1,312	1 to 398
2000	527,285	906	1 to 581
2005	420,423	850	1 to 495

While the figures show an improvement in the ratio between 2000 and 2005, it may be that the worst is yet to come. Given that the young clergy of today emerged from the pool of youth who were in high school seven or more years ago, there is lag time to consider. Because of the significant drop in youth involvement (at least in church school) since 2000, the pool of youth from which future young clergy will emerge is even smaller than the pool that produced today's meager number of young clergy. Another factor to consider is that with fewer young clergy as role models, today's youth may be even less inclined to see ordained ministry as a viable option. In this sense, the problem has a self-perpetuating aspect.

An even more troubling prospect comes when one sees that the decline in children in church school has been more pronounced than the decline in youth; there likely will be fewer children moving into the youth ministries of churches from which most of the young clergy come. In the case of both children and youth, United Methodism in the United States has been reaching a smaller and smaller percentage of children and youth in the population for a number of years.

A first, critical step in stemming the tide of the young clergy crisis is, therefore, to increase the volume of youth meaningfully engaged in church. This means taking a hard look at the format of current youth programs and finding ways to increase their attractiveness, relevance, and energy level. It also means finding the resources and the willingness within graying congregations to prioritize youth ministry, to open doors to youth beyond the congregation, to listen and respond to the spiritual needs of young people today, and to engage them in worship and leadership roles.

Unfortunately, many congregations fall short in this area. One of the conclusions of a denominational State of the Church Report issued in 2007 was "while church leaders express a high level of desire to attract young people ages 18–30, they indicate less willingness to change practices and invest money in doing so."[5] This assessment can be expanded to apply to those in the younger teenage years as well: "Youth ministry is a ministry on the margins," laments a young clergy. "There is a sense that youth ministry is a less-than ministry in the local church and on the Conference level. It is something you pass through on your way to other more important ministries in the local church and on the Conference level.... We don't put emphasis and value in youth ministry."

Recent sociological research on the spiritual life of American teenagers suggests that many churches may be missing the mark when it comes to developing the faith of adolescents. There is an urgent need for congregations to take more seriously the spiritual lives of young persons, to present them with a compelling theology, and to engage them meaningfully.

Research also affirms that parental influence is a primary influence on children's religious beliefs, even for older teenagers. Successful youth ministries must enlist parents as key allies, educating and equipping them to model faithful living and nurture the spiritual formation of their own children. The best way to get youth involved and serious about faith is to get their parents involved and serious.[6] Work with parents may not be easy in some cases. As one committed and active layperson said in responding to the decreasing numbers of young clergy, "As important as I know young clergy are to the future of the church, I have to admit that I would have mixed feelings if one of my children decided to enter ordained ministry. I would be concerned about what kind of future they would have."

While youth clearly want, and need, fun social interaction, youth ministry is more than fun and games. As noted earlier, 88 percent of young United Methodist elders report that at least one adult had taken them seriously when they were youth. Sociologist of religion Carol Lytch, who has researched the question of what connects kids with church, concludes that a sense of belonging, the search for meaning, and the opportunity to develop competence are the three hooks attracting youth to church.[7] Youth ministry expert Kenda Creasy Dean identifies the need to feel part of something great as a fundamental characteristic of adolescence.[8] Compelling, well-directed youth ministry connects with young people along these critical dimensions. And part of taking youth seriously includes a genuine willingness to share leadership with them and give young persons serious responsibilities, so they can experience what it means to be in active ministry.

Finally, youth ministry needs to induct young people into an ongoing practice of discernment regarding the broad issue of vocation. While vocation is not the primary focus of any youth program, it "deserves a place at the table" within the broader agenda of spiritual formation and Christian identity.[9] Some congregations have developed structured programs to introduce the subject of vocational call within the context of youth ministry. Sometimes, it is less a matter of having a formal program, and more a matter of raising the subject of ordained ministry and finding ways to extend the invitation explicitly. The Fund for Theological Education, out of their work in assisting congregations with enlistment, has developed a list of practices congregations may use. (The list is found at the end of this chapter.)

Increasing the effectiveness of campus ministry is another urgent priority. Once young people graduate from high school, "they drop out of church in huge numbers," says the Reverend Frank Wulf, pastor of United University Church on the University of Southern California campus. "Most universities are not very friendly to organized religion."[10] Wulf calls on individuals and congregations to support campus ministries in their area by volunteering to serve on the board of directors, by inviting campus ministers to preach in their pulpits, by exploring possibilities for cooperative or cluster ministries for young people, and by actively keeping in touch with their own college students.[11] A number of church-related colleges have used Lilly Endowment grants to engage students with vocational discernment. Many of these include campus ministry as an integral part of their programs.

No increase in the number of young persons entering ministry can be sustained in the long run unless the denomination and individual congregations prioritize ministry with young persons—starting with children and youth and continuing through the college years. This renewal must broaden the numbers of young persons involved and deepen their spiritual nurture.

Without this, no efforts to recruit 22-year-olds to seminary or entice college students to exploration events, no adjustments to clergy salaries or simplification of ordination procedures will be sufficient to draw more young persons into our pulpits.

But let us remember, too, that we are called to reach young persons for Christ, not merely to address a potential personnel shortage, but because God's heart longs for the hearts of today's children and youth. If the young clergy crisis is what it takes to motivate the denomination to reach out to more young persons and develop their faith, then it may be that God is guiding us to wrestle many blessings out of the crisis we face.

Ten Practices for Nurturing the Next Generation of Pastoral Leaders

1. Adopt the practice of regularly and consistently inviting young people to consider pastoral ministry as a profession.
2. Take the initiative to speak directly to a young person about their gifts for ministry.
3. Use confirmation class as an opportunity to ask the question, "What will you do with your life in light of your faith?"
4. Give young people the opportunity to know a pastor well: the opportunity to see the person within the persona.
5. Put them into opportunities for ministry, then say the opportune word.
6. Develop eyes for the unlikely candidate (the most biblical of these practices!).
7. Be the one to hear their story—the way that they interpret and make sense of their experiences.
8. Help young people to understand and negotiate the obstacles along the path to ordination.
9. Trust the movement of the Holy Spirit and trust that God will provide leaders for the Church.
10. Develop a sense for who is truly gifted for pastoral ministry and who simply needs a deeper experience of discipleship.[12]

CHAPTER SIX

The Entry Process

Ordained ministry is recognized by The United Methodist Church as a called-out and set-apart ministry. Therefore, it is appropriate that those persons who present themselves as candidates for licensed or ordained ministry be examined regarding the authenticity of their call by God to ordered ministry.
2004 United Methodist Book of Discipline, ¶ 310

Integral to the understanding of ordained ministry in the United Methodist Church is the annual conference's role in examining and approving those seeking ordination and overseeing their preparation for ministry. Individuals discerning a call to ministry are required to take part in a process designed to ensure that they are genuinely called and sincerely faithful, that they are psychologically and educationally prepared for the rigors of ministry, and that they are fruitful and effective in service.

How does the ordination process relate to the young clergy situation? There is no simple answer to that question. Candidacy and ordination processes are multifaceted, and many different players are involved. Practices can vary from conference to conference, and the length of time candidates spend in the process can vary significantly. So it is difficult to generalize about the process. Young clergy tend to perceive some parts of the candidacy and ordination process as encouraging, while other aspects are perceived as discouraging.

Background on the Probationary Process

In 1996, the General Conference approved a new probationary process for candidates seeking ordination in the denomination. Under the new legislation, a candidate seeking ordination is commissioned following the completion of educational and other requirements. The commissioned minister then enters a probationary period of at least three years under the supervision and guidance of the person's annual conference board of ordained ministry.

The concept of a probationary period was not new in United Methodism. In 1996, the standard probationary period was two years. A major emphasis of the advocates of the 1996 legislation was that of a "new" understanding of the probationary period, not merely the adding of an additional year to the current probationary period. The legislation clarified what was expected to take place during the longer probationary period. The current (2004) *Book of Discipline of The United Methodist Church* describes the process as follows:

> ¶ **326.** *Probationary Service of Commissioned Ministers*—All persons who are commissioned ministers shall be appointed by a bishop (¶ 430) and serve a minimum of three years following the completion of education requirements for full connection as a probationary member of the annual conference. During the probationary period, arrangements shall be offered by the board of ordained ministry for all commissioned ministers to be involved in a curriculum that extends theological education by using covenant groups and mentoring to support the practice and work of their ministry as servant leaders, to contemplate the grounding of ordained ministry, and to understand covenant ministry in the life of the conference. The specialized service of probationary members shall be evaluated by the

> district superintendent and the board of ordained ministry in terms of the probationary member's ability to express and give leadership in servant ministry.

The General Board of Higher Education and Ministry, through its Division of Ordained Ministry, was charged with establishing the recommended guidelines for annual conference boards of ordained ministry to use in developing their respective probationary programs. *Principles and Guides for Annual Conferences* recommends four dimensions: supervision, continuing theological education, mentoring, and covenant groups.

Encouraging Aspects of Candidacy and Ordination

Results of the Lewis Center survey show that young clergy find mentoring to be the most positive part of the candidacy and ordination processes. This finding is consistent with the results of prior Lewis Center research on the effectiveness of the United Methodist probationary process. This research, conducted with all those ordained over a five-year period beginning in 1999, concluded that mentoring is overwhelmingly positive for most probationers and that mentoring should be put front and center in the probationary process.[1]

The opportunity to spend time with others who are just entering ministry is also perceived as a positive aspect of the process by many. Young clergy value the collegiality and new relationships built among their peers. Again and again, young clergy's survey responses reflected the need they feel to be together with others their age.

Many survey respondents felt that another positive aspect of the process was the encouragement they received as younger candidates. One respondent said, "I felt that people wanted me to succeed. I was viewed as a breath of fresh air." While some young clergy felt their age was a disadvantage in the entry process, they were in the minority.

Discouraging Aspects of Candidacy and Ordination

On the negative side, the length of the process stands well above all other concerns. Some young clergy lamented the fact that the process can feel negative and mean-spirited. Some even likened it to a form of hazing. Others objected to the process as overly bureaucratic, politicized, and laden with red tape. "I found that too many aspects of the process are more like hoops to jump through rather than a spiritually supportive process of growth," said one young clergyperson. Others said they found the system inconsistent and confusing, and were distressed about unclear expectations and a lack of communication.

It is clear from the survey that some young clergy view candidacy and ordination procedures as a major stumbling block to young persons entering ministry. Among the respondents, 40 percent said they had considered seeking ordination in a different denomination at some point during the candidacy and ordination process. When asked why, reasons having to do with the length of, and frustration with, the ordination process exceeded all others. When asked the question "What one change in the UMC would make it more attractive to potential young clergy?" responses related to *streamlining the candidacy process* were the second mostly frequently offered, just behind issues having to do with the appointment process.

Too Much Expected of the Entry Process

Over many years, the process of entry into ordained ministry has gotten longer and much more involved. The church has probably put too much weight on the entry process. There is a sense in which the church is asking boards of ordained ministry to solve problems not of their making. For example, the impact of continuing membership loss and concern for ineffective clergy causes more pressure to be put on those who screen new clergy. The new clergy often feel that they are paying the price for the failure of others. Unfortunately, instead of addressing these church problems directly with those who have been responsible in the past decades, there is a misguided hope that examining new clergy closely enough will compensate for problems caused by some current clergy. Some have suggested, only half jokingly, that we keep the board of ordained ministry to deal with entering clergy but establish a *board of already ordained ministry* to address the issues within the ranks of existing clergy.

An example of the increasing pressure put on the entry process is found in the amount of the *Discipline* devoted to the candidacy and ordination process. In 1968, when The United Methodist Church was formed, 43 pages were devoted to this subject. By 2004, the number of pages needed to cover the process was 90 pages. One major factor leading to the pressure on the entry process is what is usually referred to as guaranteed appointments for elders. If there were no guaranteed appointments, the entry process would not have to carry so much weight. If there were better ways to deal with ineffectiveness after ordination, then much less would be at stake in the entry process.

What can be done to improve the entry process and make it more encouraging and helpful to potential young clergy? In general, conferences should work toward an approach that is more positive in tone, more focused on the development of the individual, and more welcoming to young persons.

Rename and Reframe the Probationary Process

Wanting to clarify her understanding of the steps into ordained ministry, a first-year seminarian engaged one of her professors in a conversation. She had just been home for Thanksgiving and had met with her district superintendent. To be sure that she understood the process the superintendent had outlined, she reviewed the conversation with her professor. She proceeded to explain her understanding of the steps. But she showed some hesitancy in talking about what happens after graduation. "Following seminary I will be eligible for commissioning and will be put on probation," she said with some doubt in her voice. The professor assured her she was correct. She replied, "Probation? That's what my brother got when he broke into a neighbor's house."

Her story illustrates the problem with the language used in the ordination process. While phrases such as "on trial" or "on probation" are historically meaningful in United Methodist polity, they communicate something very negative for emerging generations. To young people, this kind of language carries connotations of the criminal justice system and not anything remotely associated with spirituality. Young persons not sure about what it meant to be on probation would probably turn first to an Internet search. And the first results they would find would likely be: American Probation and Parole Association, Department of Probation, Juvenile Probation Commission, Federal Probation, and U.S. Probation and Pretrial Services! The church can surely find language that better reflects what we mean by *probation*.

It is distressing that the current probationary process is experienced by many as a set of requirements rather than an opportunity for development. In ecumenical circles, the United Methodist probationary process is thought of as the gold standard among denominations. Most denominations are working to incorporate one or two elements of the process into their systems, but are finding it hard because their polities are less connectional. They often are envious of the United Methodist plan.

It would help both boards and probationers if the valuable individual components of the process could be framed in a larger vision that has the probationer, not the board or conference, at the center. An individual well versed in mentoring in secular settings was once asked what she thought about the United Methodist probationary process. She said, "It sounds as if the board of ordained ministry is saying to new probationers that we have put in place all these things to ensure that you will be ready for ordination within three years." Unfortunately, however, that is not often how either boards or probationers view the process.

How might things be different if the dominant philosophy of the process were preparing the candidate for ordination? The boards would design everything around the goal of ensuring that those who have already been deemed to have "readiness for ministry" at commissioning will be able to demonstrate "effectiveness in ministry" in time for ordination. Probationers would see, in everything that is done and said, that the process is for them, not for the board or conference. The end result would then best serve the conference and the church at large as well.

Such reframing would contribute to building trust among all participants. This is an important goal since all else depends on the establishment of trust. From the beginning of this process for growth and development, conferences need to allow probationer input into the content of the program. They should view every expectation from the perspective of the probationers and ask, "Is this aspect of the process helping to move the candidate from readiness to effectiveness?" It is also crucial for boards to review procedures to be sure that they communicate a sense of caring and encouragement and that they develop quality relationships. Finally, they should strive for quality and accountability in the leadership of all aspects of the process and work to develop open and effective channels of communication among all participants.

Put Mentoring Front and Center

All of the Lewis Center's research points to the conclusion that mentoring has more potential to develop effectiveness in those entering ministry than any other component of the process. Conferences should be encouraged to emphasize this aspect of the process and develop their mentoring programs so that they live up to their potential.

One aspect of a successful mentoring program is choosing the right individuals as mentors. Good mentors should be able to serve as positive role models, share information that helps the probationer grow in effectiveness, and give guidance in the probationer's congregational, conference, and denominational ministry development. While probationers would like to have input into the selection of mentors, the most important criteria in assigning mentors may be quality, fit, and willingness. Karen

Koons, a young pastor in Mississippi, talked, often informally, with young colleagues about their mentors. They told her effective mentors "took them by the hand and showed the way" and "stayed in touch afterwards." Young clergy are not asking for coddling; they may, however, need direction if they are going to move to effectiveness.

Mentoring is most effective when mentors are clear about their role and value the process. Providing adequate training for mentors and orientation for those being mentored is an important step toward such clarity. The effectiveness of the mentoring relationship also improves when there is stability, accountability, and regular communication. All of these factors build trust and respect, both of which are key to the success of mentoring.

Avoid Ageism

Of the young clergy polled by the Lewis Center, 46 percent felt that their age was not an issue when they went through the candidacy and ordination process. The next largest group, 36 percent, felt it was an advantage. But there was a significant minority of 19 percent who felt they were disadvantaged in the process by their young age. "In spite of the general agreement that the church needs more young leaders," said one, "most laypeople, including those on the Board of Ordained Ministry, seem to prefer a middle-aged man as their pastor."

Some young clergy report being asked questions not asked of older candidates, such as "How old are you?", "Do you have a family?", and "Do you feel mature enough to pastor a congregation?" A 26-year-old single woman seeking ordination, wrote in her blog, "Throughout my candidacy process, I constantly ran into places where the process clearly was meant for those who were second-career, and already serving churches as local pastors during candidacy. I run into people who ask if I have a family—I say yes, I have family that lives nearby, and they tell me: 'No, I mean a family of *your own*.' "[2]

These kinds of questions, often asked quite innocently by well-intentioned committee members, can make younger candidates feel unwelcome, unsure of themselves, and out of place. Local staff-parish relations committees, boards of ordained ministry, and others who interface with ministry candidates should be trained to avoid subtle expressions of ageism and questions that would be out of bounds in any other type of job interview.

It behooves everyone involved in the entry process—congregational leaders, conference officials, and candidates—to remember that the purpose of the process is preparation for ministry. Keeping that objective paramount is essential to making the experiences of candidacy and steps toward ordination positive and productive for all, particularly for young clergy.

CHAPTER SEVEN

The Need to Support Young Clergy

The church has very high expectations of young clergy. They expect us to save a declining church, but we are given a very short leash if what we are proposing has never been done before.
Daniel Mejia, young pastor, Maryland

The reality of so few young clergy is more than statistics on a page. It often involves young clergy feeling alienated, alone, and unsupported among clergy colleagues old enough to be their parents or grandparents. Many serve aging congregations that are wary of their youthfulness and skeptical about change, yet, at the same time, expect their young ministers to restore declining congregations to their former glory. Often young clergy have very few contemporaries in their congregations, districts, and conferences.

Andrew C. Thompson, a thoughtful commentator on Gen X issues, calls isolation the "plague of our generation." He feels that his generation's isolation is compounded many times for young clergy. Thompson cites conversations with a Gen X colleague from Arkansas, Eric Van Meter, who identifies some of the reasons.

Young clergy tend to move more frequently than their older counterparts, thus making it harder to establish deep roots and relationships. At the same time that new clergy are trying to establish their pastoral identity, they often do not have peer groups, especially following the probationary process and ordination.[1]

Geographical isolation is another reality. Young clergy find themselves separated from support systems developed in their seminary years, but not yet connected with well-established clergy networks within their conferences. This is particularly the case for clergy who attended seminary farther from home or who enter conferences with few seminary classmates.

To a young elder in the Southeast, the reality hit home when he would attend district clergy events with his wife and young children. He could not find any other clergy in his district who had children in grade school, or even any children still at home. "There really wasn't much affirmation for people who were just coming in. There wasn't any network or support for us, no understanding of what we should get involved in. I found myself praying for the sense that the church really wanted me and was willing to make a long-term investment in me."

Even when young clergy have colleagues within their conferences, geographical isolation can make getting together difficult. It is not uncommon for an annual conference covering a huge geographical area to have only five or six probationary or ordained elders under 35. As one Midwestern clergywoman put it, "I have to go to an event halfway across the country to be together with 20 or more young clergy." A probationer from the Northeast laments, "When I am ordained in a couple of years, I will be the only elder under 30 in my conference."

In the Lewis Center survey, young clergy indicated that one of the most valuable aspects of the candidacy and probationary process is the opportunity for young clergy to be together with colleagues. However, after ordination, this opportunity often evaporates. In answer to the question, "What one thing could your annual conference do to be more supportive of young clergy," providing opportunities for young clergy to gather was one of the most common responses. The need for a peer support system is a sentiment echoed over and over by today's young clergy. They know they must take responsibility for developing their own support systems, but they also would welcome conference assistance. The demands of ministry, family, and child care responsibilities; distance; and lack of authority make it difficult for the young clergy themselves to initiate and carry out such events.

Importance of Place

Emerging generations put a tremendous importance on place. Cities and states understand this reality. Some localities attract and keep young adults by providing events that bring together young workers in their communities to meet one another and connect with volunteer opportunities. It has been said that the majority of Gen Xers put more value on a good place to live than on a good job.

Some young clergy feel an uncomfortable dislocation in communities that are very different from those they might choose for themselves. Young clergy's acceptance of itineracy is strained when they feel a loss of control over their destiny or fear going to a locale where they will be isolated from much that is important for them.

For some young pastors, particularly those serving in rural areas, there is loneliness and social isolation. They are often appointed to serve in congregations where their own generation is totally absent within the membership and, sometimes, largely absent in the community. Young clergy in many regions tell of early appointments that put them sometimes 50 to over 100 miles from places to shop or eat. The sense of isolation can be particularly difficult for young, single clergy, and it may be one reason that singles are so underrepresented among young, United Methodist clergy compared to the general population of 25- to 34-year-olds. Only about 21 percent of young, single clergy agreed with the statement "I am able to date or pursue social connections"; 46 percent disagreed.

Pressured by Generational Crosscurrents

Some young clergy feel the pressure of what is sometimes called the *lifesaver mentality*. "We are expected to save the church with our energy and new ideas, but they give us very little rope," says a young clergywoman from the Midwest. "Parishioners and older colleagues express in subtle and not so subtle ways that the future of the church hinges on our ability to save it," writes another young clergywoman. "Not only does the laity look to us for a church-saving miracle but our retired and close-to-retiring colleagues also look to us to 'turn this ship around.' Within only a few years of ministry to our names, we quickly learn that great, if not impossible things are expected of us."[2]

They also feel caught between the desire to reach out to a new generation and their obligation to care for their aging congregations and institutions. A young clergywoman from Virginia put it rather bluntly: "I feel the very assignment I've been given is at odds with reaching my own generation. I could think of a hundred ways to bring young people into the church that would probably be pretty successful, but I don't get to minister to those folks. I feel like a slave to the institution I'm assigned to and can hardly get out of it."

When young pastors do succeed in bringing new, young people into their congregations, they often find themselves in the role of cross-cultural interpreters, having to bridge the gap between congregations steeped in their own institutional cultures and a new generation that often has no prior experience of church. "I find myself having to be an apologist for an institutional system that can be overwhelming for newcomers," says a young clergywoman from California.[3] "When I bring younger adults into church leadership, they are quickly overwhelmed by the maze of procedures and policies that seem to thwart actual ministry."[4] These generational crosscurrents can leave young clergy feeling drained and caught in the middle.

The Need for Support

What can help young clergy in these difficult situations? One solution is to appoint young clergy more strategically, either to communities or congregations where other young people are present or to associate pastor positions or "teaching congregations" where they will have the support of other clergy. Appointment issues are discussed at length in the next chapter.

The ability to be in a community with other young clergy can help young clergy navigate this difficult terrain. Conferences should provide opportunities for young clergy to come together. But since many conferences have a very small number of pastors under the age of 35, young clergy need to be connected with those beyond their conference as well. Jurisdictions, denominational agencies, seminaries, and other organizations should look for opportunities to support young clergy by providing fellowship, learning, and leadership development opportunities.

The Lewis Fellows Program

Since 2005, the Lewis Center for Church Leadership has been conducting a pilot program called the Lewis Fellows that brings together groups of outstanding young clergypersons from around the country for an ongoing program of intensive leadership development. This program is supported through the Sustaining Pastoral Excellence Initiative of the Lilly Endowment, Inc. The groups come together periodically over two years.

Participants in this program have found the opportunities for peer interaction and support to be invaluable. "Every time we gather, within the first few moments, I feel community," said a member of the inaugural group of Lewis Fellows. "This is the only clergy gathering I've been a part of with no acrimony or backbiting. There has been real trust." Over two years, the Lewis Fellows forged extraordinary friendships and a network of professional accountability and support. "I don't feel alone anymore," one Lewis Fellow said of his experience.

But the program involves more than building community and fellowship. The emphasis is on leadership development and encouraging fruitfulness in ministry. Such leadership training for young clergy is particularly important. Because of the dearth of clergy leaders in their generation, many of today's young clergy will be called to serve in challenging situations much earlier than clergy in previous generations. Of the graduates of the first Lewis Fellows cohort, one is stepping into a senior position of denominational leadership in the Christian Church (Disciples of Christ). One has launched a successful satellite worship service. One is planting a new church. And another was elected to public office while continuing to serve his congregation. Several Lewis Fellows were elected as clergy delegates to General Conference for 2004 and 2008. All of these clergy are in their 20s and 30s. Many other young clergy could benefit from this type of program if the opportunities were available.

More Support Needed

Bishops, superintendents, local pastor-parish relations committees, and other church leaders all must be mindful of the need to support and encourage young clergy in this era of isolation, pressure, and high expectations. We are aware of several conferences that have planned special events for young clergy or have given young clergy the opportunity to work together as a team in the context of ongoing connectional responsibilities. More of this is needed. Mentoring, discussed in the previous chapter, is another important component of support. Simply giving young clergy the opportunity to be heard will help increase the awareness of the unique challenges they face in ministry, and increased awareness is the first step toward a more hospitable climate for the young.

CHAPTER EIGHT

Deployment of Young Clergy

The first appointment for young clergy is essential to success and longevity. . . . We have to make first appointments for young clergy be a culture of development. . . . And, we need to identify churches that are willing to . . . see the development of young clergy spiritual leadership as part of their mission as followers of Jesus.

Erika Gara, young clergy pastor and blogger

"Let no [one] despise thy youth," said Paul to Timothy; but I doubt whether that advice stopped any of the old saints from wagging their heads.[1]

Reinhold Niebuhr, age 23

While many young clergy feel that their appointments are a good fit with their gifts for ministry, a significant group would agree with Lyle Schaller that too often "talented ministers are 'set up to fail' by being invited to serve churches where their gifts, skills, experience, personality, and other characteristics do not match the needs and culture of that congregation at this point in its history."[2] The result, too often, is disillusioned pastors and unhappy members. Schaller believes that the placement of all clergy is far more difficult today than in previous generations—but this is especially true for young clergy. Despite the difficulties, Schaller contends that a placement system that matches all pastors and congregations well is a cost-beneficial strategy that could turn the denomination around.[3]

More strategic deployment of young clergy is arguably the best way the denomination can use the scarce resource of young leadership to enhance its outreach among younger generations, while at the same time helping young clergy survive and thrive in ministry. In the opinion of those responding to the Lewis Center's survey, the single most important thing conferences can do to support young clergy is to pay more attention to first and second appointments.

Pay Attention to Young Clergy Appointments

Recently, a group of United Methodist bishops met with David McAllister-Wilson, president of Wesley Theological Seminary, to discuss the declining number of young elders. When they asked McAllister-Wilson, "What can be done?" he turned the question back to them. "When you made your appointments this year," he asked, "at what point in the process were the appointments for the young coming out of seminary considered?" The bishops replied that these appointments are usually made last; that is how the system tends to work.

When bishops and cabinets do not consider the appointment of young clergy until the very end of the process, the options are severely limited. "It may be that we can no longer afford to operate this way in the future," said McAllister-Wilson. "If young clergy are indeed our 'endangered species,' then it follows that attention needs to be given to them earlier in the process when a broader range of options is available." There may be other clergy needing special attention in the appointment process, but young clergy certainly do as well.

McAllister-Wilson contends that we can no longer risk following a Friedrich Nietzsche philosophy of first appointments—what doesn't kill you makes you stronger. "We cannot afford to 'eat our seed corn,' " he cautions.

First and second appointments are critical junctures for clergy who are just beginning ministry. Such transitions are very vulnerable times for anyone, but young clergy are particularly vulnerable because they are experiencing multiple transitions simultaneously. Not only are they facing the normal transition all pastors face going into a new congregation, they are also transitioning from seminary, moving into their first full-time ministry context, and beginning a calling for which they have been prepared by education but, often, not yet by experience. At best, their experience in ministry has been part-time.

When conference leaders consider how young clergy should be deployed, phrases that often come up are "paying your dues," "marking time," and "waiting your turn." "Didn't we have to do these things?" older clergy may ask. It is true that historically younger clergy spent a number of years in some of the same churches to which they are appointed today. Thirty years ago, however, many of these churches were thriving. Now, after suffering decades of decline, they are less adaptable and resilient and less open to young leadership.

Another difference is that when the first of the baby boomers were young clergy, virtually all the clergy were men. If they were married, their spouses either did not work outside the home or they worked in professions that could be practiced in most locales, such as teaching or nursing. This is not the case for most young clergy today, who may have more difficulty accepting certain appointments because of their spouse's employment.

Moreover, in previous generations many, if not most, clergy came from rural or small membership and small town congregations. That was where a large portion of the denomination's membership was. So when young clergy were assigned to these types of churches, they were likely to be familiar with the setting. Today most clergy come from large membership or suburban churches. Congregational life in many of the churches to which they are assigned bears no resemblance to what they have previously experienced.

In addition to these challenges, the tremendous age difference between young clergy and their congregants in smaller, aging congregations intensifies the experience of culture shock. It is hard for the young clergy to know how to lead and hard for the congregations to accept the young clergy as leaders. "My church members were not even the age of my parents. The youngest ones were the age of my grandparents. A whole generation, almost two, was missing," says one new pastor.

Appoint Young Clergy Where They Can Make a Difference

Young clergy may be the denomination's last, best hope for connecting with the emerging generation that is so often underrepresented in our churches today. Young clergy understand the imperative of reaching out to their own generation and are eager to do so, but they feel hemmed in by the obligations of ministering to their aging flocks and maintaining aging institutions. "I spend so much time ministering to people substantially older than me," says a young clergyman from the Mid-Atlantic region, "that it's hard to even find time to minister to people my own age." This is especially true in the smaller, less vital congregations to which first appointments are often made. Another young pastor from the West says that, even if there were young people in the communities to reach, "we are too exhausted to reach them because of the heavy expectations and demands of an aging congregation for pastoral care."

As one clergywoman put it, "I left seminary with a heart for reaching the young. But after three appointments that gave me no opportunity to do so, I am now in a church with potential. However, I am no longer young and now have family responsibilities that make it harder than before to be available at the hours needed to reach the young." There is little logic in assigning the youngest clergy to communities where the fewest young adults are present—although this is very often what happens.

"Churches get the pastors they can afford, not the pastors they really need," reflects one young pastor. "And so we send young clergy into mostly dead churches hoping they can pull a Jesus-raising-Lazarus kind of miracle."

Use Associate Positions Strategically

Serving as an associate pastor can be an excellent way for a young clergyperson to learn good skills and practices during the early years of ministry. Although many young clergy are interested in being appointed to their own churches, there also are many who express the desire to serve as associates. Whenever possible, conferences should try to honor that preference. In some conferences, where smaller churches are more the norm, few associate positions are available. But overall, about 40 percent of young elders today are serving as associates.

Unfortunately, some young clergy who go into associate positions hoping the experience will be one of growth and development are disappointed. Many young associate pastors who shared their experiences with the Lewis Center registered complaints about the senior pastors with whom they serve. It is clear that conferences need to take great care in selecting the senior pastors with whom young associates serve. There is little that an associate can learn from a poor senior pastor.

And even gifted and effective senior pastors are often ill prepared to work with an associate. Training for such pastors would help them be more effective as mentors, coaches, and teachers. A senior pastor in California said that she had worked with a series of young associates before she realized that she was assuming far too much about the level of knowledge, experience, and maturity of those associates. Once she learned a better way of working with her clergy staff colleagues, they both flourished and so did the congregation.

The value of a strong example and mentor is seen in the account of a young man who attended seminary in Washington, D.C. His father contacted H. Beecher Hicks Jr., longtime pastor of Metropolitan Baptist Church in Washington, who was an old friend. He asked if there was work his son could do at Metropolitan to gain ministry experience during his seminary years. The only position Dr. Hicks could find for the young man was to be his driver. As it turned out, the young man learned much from this legendary leader and preacher over the next three years, even though his work involved little professional responsibility, because Beecher was such an effective mentor, coach, and teacher.

Young clergy report that conferences tend to have different patterns with respect to how they treat associates when it is time for them to move to their second appointments. The perception is that in some conferences associates tend to get greater salary increases in the early years because they serve congregations that will use their greater resources to prevent them from looking elsewhere. In their next appointments these associates will then tend to move to a larger church that offers a larger salary than what their colleagues are earning when they serve as solo pastors in their first appointments. However, there is a perception in other conferences that associate years do not seem to count in the same way as do years serving as a solo pastor. Thus, associates may have to take a pay cut to go to a church of their own, especially if their salary has gotten out of alignment with those with whom they entered the conference.

While neither scenario may actually be the case consistently within conferences, cabinets will need to be sensitive to these dynamics and not prejudice either type of first appointment. Both are important and should be entered not because of advancement opportunities or resisted because of downsides, but because that is where the new clergy can best serve and learn.

Some conferences have fewer associate positions and fewer healthy churches today, thus increasing the challenge their cabinets face in finding the early placements that truly provide the culture of development so needed. Strong congregations with strong leadership should be encouraged to understand that part of their mission can be as incubators for new leaders. Some of the denomination's largest and most effective congregations have the capacity to serve as teaching congregations, receiving more than one young associate each year. This type of a situation gives the associates a valuable opportunity to learn within the context of an effective ministry environment, while at the same time serving alongside other young clergy.

Conferences should also try to avoid making assumptions about the types of ministry that interest young clergy. While some young clergy want to do youth ministry, others resent the assumption that because they are young they should be working with youth. For every young clergyperson who feels called to youth ministry, there are others who feel quite ungifted for such work. As one person put it, "Not all young medical doctors become pediatricians!"

What about Giving the Young Really Good Appointments?

The notion of waiting one's turn is so ingrained in many conferences' cultures that varying from this norm in any way can attract attention and cause concern. When bishops and cabinets have made bold appointments of the young to churches normally served by older clergy, they quickly learn what it feels like to receive the ire of other clergy. One veteran pastor complained that the salaries of "seasoned baby boomer thinkers and solid liturgical worship leaders" are being cut in favor of "younger, more charismatic personalities, who are sure to entertain, yet don't have the experience to be senior ministers to the particular churches to which they are being sent." Such sentiments need to be countered with the argument that young clergy are capable of great ministry achievements.

Clergy and cabinets also need to keep in mind that the number of young clergy in most conferences is very small. Very few older clergy would be disadvantaged or displaced if the most capable young received fitting appointments.

It is also important to recognize that most of today's young clergy will be called to serve in challenging situations much earlier than young clergy in previous generations, because of the number of baby boomers who are retiring. This means that they need to get good experience fast. Too often young clergy are sent to the least desirable, most problematic churches simply because they are the ones lowest in the system. When appointed to a dysfunctional congregation in their first or second appointment, new clergy cannot learn what is needed to lead effectively. In fact, they are likely to acquire bad habits that must be unlearned later if they are to reach emerging generations for Christ. The denomination can ill afford having its scarce resource of young clergy spending years marking time in dysfunctional and problematic ministry settings.

Extra care should be taken to appoint young clergy to supportive and healthy churches. And churches receiving young pastors need some coaching and training in how to work with and support a young pastor, since fewer and fewer congregations today are practiced in working with younger leadership.

Itineracy—the Elephant in the Room

Most United Methodists show little nostalgia for the older system of making appointments in which pastors only learned their assignments when they were read by the bishop on the last day of annual conference. In the South, years ago, there was a custom of the pastors standing around the altar rail for the reading of those appointments. As each name was read, the pastor would step forward and the bishop would read the appointment for the coming year. The tradition was that the pastor would then reply upon hearing the appointment (for the first time!), "God is good. Thank you, Bishop." However, there was once a pastor who had just moved the year before and was hoping not to move again that particular year. When the bishop read another appointment for him, the pastor was so taken aback that he forgot what he was supposed to say and exclaimed, "Good God, Bishop!"

Many look back on that era with some disdain and even wonder how pastors could have submitted to a system that gave them such little involvement. Yet, for the most part they did accept the system without many of the misgivings we now have about this approach to itineracy. The story illustrates that the system of itineracy has not been static; it has changed significantly in the last generation because of resistance to the older scheme. Understandings of what constitutes itineracy continue to evolve generation by generation. And they are likely to continue to evolve in light of continued pressures and concerns.

The emerging generation of United Methodist elders does not think the system of itineracy works well. Less than 5 percent of young elders responding to the Lewis Center's survey strongly agreed with the statement, "Itineracy as practiced today is working well." This does not mean, however, that younger clergy want to go to a congregational call system. Very few felt that congregations should select their pastors from a list provided by the conference.

Guaranteed Appointments

Young clergy are not strong advocates of the practice of guaranteed appointments. Many name it as contributing to the church's problem with ineffective clergy. Most young clergy are not attracted to the idea of being part of a "clergy union," and are quite willing to serve without such "protection." They are discouraged by the union mentality that appears to make years of service the only relevant factor in salaries, rather than how well or how poorly one serves in ministry.

In a document drafted by a Council of Bishops task force in 2007, the history of the guaranteed appointment is traced, beginning with its addition in The Methodist Church in 1956 as a deliberate limitation to the power of the episcopacy. It was intended to restrain arbitrary, sexist, or racist abuses of authority. "Every traveling preacher, unless retired, supernumerary, on sabbatical leave, or under arrest of character, must receive an appointment" (1956 *Discipline*). In 1968, with the union of the Evangelical United Brethren and Methodists to form The United Methodist Church, what had been listed as a limitation on the powers of the episcopacy became a right of those in itineracy. "Every effective member in full connection who is in good standing in an annual conference shall receive an annual appointment by the bishop" (1968 *Discipline*). Current language in the *Discipline* is quite similar: "Every effective elder in full connection who is in good standing shall be continued under appointment by the bishop" (2004 *Discipline*, ¶ 334.1).

The bishops and others are seeking to make changes in 2008 that will still guard against episcopal abuses, while maintaining board of ordained ministry prerogatives in deciding who is qualified for ordained ministry, and at the same time these changes will serve to take away the protection that guaranteed appointments have given to ineffective pastors. Currently, the burden rests with the bishop and cabinet to demonstrate evidence of ineffectiveness. The suggested changes would shift the burden to the pastor to provide continuing evidence of effectiveness as defined by the annual conference. Guaranteed appointment would thereby move from a right of clergy to a privilege that requires evidence of growth in vocational competence and effectiveness, and a willingness to accept the missional strategy of the bishop that is reflected in the appointment process.

We believe that such a change would serve young clergy well. They are more than willing to be accountable to a common set of criteria that are fairly administered. They want to grow; they expect to grow. But they want to feel they are a part of a covenant where they are not the only ones expected to improve. They expect accountability throughout the system, including from those who have more responsibility and privilege within the conference.

Appointing young clergy with care, in ways that support their development, reward their effort, and make good use of both their ministry gifts and youthfulness is perhaps the most important thing that can be done to improve the situation that young clergy confront today.

CHAPTER NINE

The Adequacy of Salaries

No one got into ministry to get rich. But all of us need to pay bills, provide for our families, and pay our student loans.[1]
Peter Cammarano, young clergy pastor and blogger

The issue of salary comes up frequently in discussions about young clergy, and, like other young clergy issues, it is varied and complex. An ecumenical group of church pension administrators, for example, registered the opinion that improving compensation was one of the most important things that could be done to reverse the decline in the number of young pastors. "Pay young clergy salaries that are comparable with their educational contemporaries," said one, "and offer good benefits so that young clergy and their families can live well." One young clergyperson says the reason there are so few young clergy is, "It's too expensive. I borrowed $50,000 for seminary and my bachelor's degree, for a job that pays $32,000." Another young clergy asserts in his blog that low salaries are part of the reason young pastors are "leaving in droves."[2]

While there is a great deal of talk about salaries, particularly in the blogosphere, it is less clear how salaries relate to the young clergy shortage. The blogger's assertion that young clergy are "leaving in droves," for example, is not represented by data on attrition that have been assembled by the Lewis Center. What evidence does seem to suggest is that the financial situation of young clergy varies greatly. Most young clergy are doing fairly well financially, but not all. A minority of about 20 percent of United Methodist young elders in the United States seem to be struggling financially.

Salary—Adequate But Not for All

Most young elders responding to the Lewis Center survey conveyed reasonably positive attitudes about salary. In response to the statement "I receive adequate salary and benefits to provide for myself and others for whom I am responsible," 50 percent agreed or strongly agreed, 29 percent gave a neutral response, and 21 percent disagreed or disagreed strongly. Asked if financial struggles hindered their ability to minister effectively, 59 percent disagreed, 22 percent were neutral, and 19 percent agreed.

A significant number (41 percent) said that financial struggles cause stress and tension for them and their families. But according to the American Psychological Association, money is the top source of stress among all American adults.[3] So the percentage of young clergy and their families experiencing financial stress is probably no more, and may in fact be less, than average. Taken together, these responses would indicate that at least half of young clergy are doing reasonably well financially, but about 20 percent are having a difficult time.

The financial well-being of any particular young clergyperson depends on a myriad of variables. Among some of the factors that influence their economic situation are salary, marital status, family size, spousal income, the financial status of their family of origin, regional cost-of-living variables, the adequacy of housing allowances in relation to the local housing market, and the presence or absence of educational or consumer debt. Because any of these factors can vary widely, the financial situation of young clergypersons can differ significantly.

Statistics from the Lewis Center's survey confirm that young elders' salaries cover a wide range. It should be noted, however, that the age and years of experience in ministry among survey respondents, who ranged in age from 25 to 35, can differ by as much as ten years.

Annual Salaries of UM Elders Age 35 and Under

Less than $25,000	8.51%
$25,000 - $29,999	14.43%
$30,000 - $34,999	33.51%
$35,000 - $39,999	21.13%
$40,000 - $44,999	12.11%
$45,000 - $49,999	5.41%
$50,000 or more	4.90%

Which young clergy are most likely to be feeling the financial pinch? We examined a number of variables to see how they related to which young clergy are more or less likely to feel their salary is adequate.

Gender

Young elder salary statistics reveal some significant similarities and disparities related to gender. Women are not more likely than men to be in the very lowest salary brackets. The percent of men and women with salaries under $30,000 is exactly the same. But moving up the salary scale, men are more likely to receive higher salaries. The Lewis Center survey indicates that 49 percent of men, but only 35 percent of women, have salaries above $35,000; and 14 percent of men have salaries above $45,000, compared to only 5 percent of women. Salary does not include housing, reimbursed expenses, or other benefits.

Young Clergy Salaries by Gender

	All Young Elders	Women	Men
Less than $30,000	23%	23%	23%
$30,000 to $34,999	36%	42%	28%
$35,000 to $44,999	33%	30%	35%
$45,000 or more	10%	5%	14%

Among the men, 56 percent agreed or strongly agreed with the statement, "I receive adequate salary and benefits to provide for myself and others for whom I am responsible." Only 43 percent of women registered that same level of agreement. Issues related to educational debt are discussed at length in the next chapter. One result that should be noted here is that the average borrowed by female United Methodist seminary graduates is 31 percent higher than for men, with single women being the most burdened by educational debt.

Marital Status

Marital status also seems to be related to financial well-being. Among the married young elders, 51 percent agreed or strongly agreed with the statement "I receive adequate salary and benefits to provide for myself and others for whom I am responsible," compared to only 48 percent of the singles. However, this distinction should be considered in light of the above gender analysis, because male young clergy are significantly more likely to be married than their female colleagues (85 percent compared to 64 percent), and women account for two-thirds of young elders who are single.

Location

Another relevant variable was the type of community in which young clergy are serving. Those in suburban communities were most likely to feel they received adequate salary and benefits, followed by those in rural areas, and then by those in towns. Those serving in urban areas were the least likely to feel their compensation was adequate.

Percent who agree strongly or very strongly with the statement, "I receive adequate salary and benefits to provide for myself and others for whom I am responsible."				
All Young Elders	**In Suburban Communities**	**In Rural Areas**	**In Towns**	**In Urban Areas**
50%	53%	50%	48%	39%

Educational Debt

One might assume that young clergy with little or no educational debt would be the most likely to find their salaries adequate. But the opposite seems to be the case. Only 28 percent of young clergy with no seminary debt and 26 percent with no college debt felt that their salary and benefits were adequate; while 46 percent of those with seminary debt of more than $30,000 and 60 percent of those with college debt over $30,000 felt their compensation was adequate. One might speculate that those with no educational debts are more likely to come from affluent families, and perhaps are used to a higher standard of living than beginning clergy salaries afford. But this hypothesis is merely speculative.

Other Variables

One variable that did not prove significant was whether young elders were serving as a solo pastor or as an associate pastor. In either type of appointment, they were equally likely to feel that their compensation is adequate. Because very few survey responses were received from elders in various racial/ethnic categories, the Lewis Center was unable to analyze race in relation to salary for elders. The Lewis Center's survey did find, however, that there are more young African Americans and Hispanics serving as deacons and local pastors than as elders, at least among survey respondents. Looking at salary figures that include all clergy, nonwhites have lower salaries, but since fewer of them are elders, that fact could be one factor explaining the differences.

Those Who Are Struggling

Twenty-three percent of young elders have salaries less than $30,000. In most ways this group is demographically representative of young clergy as a whole. The percentages of married and single, male and female, and solo and associate pastors mirror those in the overall population of young elders. But certain other variables distinguish this group, including certain financial burdens that have a much more adverse effect upon them than upon other young clergy. For example, those with salaries below $30,000 are the most likely to report having no health insurance or to be making significant payments toward their health insurance. Among the young elders with salaries below $30,000, 14 percent had no health insurance compared to 4 percent of all young elders; indeed, three-quarters of those reporting no health insurance are found in this low-salary group. About a quarter of young elders who are paying more than $6,000 per year toward their health insurance also have salaries less than $30,000 per year.

Young clergy in the lowest salary brackets have roughly the same seminary debt profile as other young clergy—about a quarter of them have seminary debts of more than $25,000. But obviously, such high levels of debt are more burdensome to those with lower salaries. And 13 percent of those with salaries under $30,000 have large undergraduate debts ($25,000 or more) compared to 8 percent of all young elders. The under $30,000 salary bracket includes 23 percent of all young elders, but 36 percent of them have undergraduate debt of more than $25,000.

When one considers that 20 percent of survey respondents in this salary bracket are single and have no second income, that single young clergy are likely to be female, and that female seminary graduates are most likely to be significantly indebted, it becomes clear how different financial factors can converge into a perfect storm of financial woes for some young clergy. While the survey data suggest that only about 20 percent of young elders are severely strained financially, their plight is very troubling, and may explain why the issue of salaries so often rises to the surface in discussions of young clergy issues.

No "One-size-fits-all" Solutions

Denominational leaders will need to be sensitive to the many variables that can affect a young pastor's financial situation and be attentive to signs of severe financial stress. All annual conferences should regularly assess their minimum salaries in light of cost-of-living changes, taking both salary and housing allowances into account, particularly in high-cost housing markets; and it is essential that they use local or regional, rather than national, cost of living figures. In addition, congregations and conference leaders need to be more aware of the growing educational debt that burdens so many recent seminary graduates.

No Ladder to Climb

This generation of young clergy is certainly not the first to confront the reality of low starting salaries for pastors. But it does appear that the emerging generation of pastors brings some different attitudes and expectations to the issue of salary than what their predecessors held. Their concerns about salary go beyond the narrow question of whether salary levels are adequate in the early years. They are concerned about the appropriateness of a salary structure built almost entirely around seniority.

One pastor with a statistical background reviewed for his conference all the variables that might be related to a pastor's salary, including such factors as payment of apportionments, growth in membership, growth in small groups, growth in worship. He said that he found there was only one statistically significant variable for salary—years of service. Whether that is the case or not, in his conference and elsewhere, there is a strong perception among young clergy that seniority is about all that matters in relation to salary level.

While to some it may seem fair to reward those with the longest service, to young clergy it sends the message that the *quality* of their leadership does not matter. Many of today's young clergy express disillusionment with the "pay your dues" and "wait your turn" mentality that governs clergy advancement.

In past generations, young pastors may have been more content to wait their turn and climb the ladder, knowing their time would eventually come. But many of today's young clergy feel that there is no longer a ladder to climb. In many conferences, large membership churches are becoming a rarity. And declining memberships and budgets in so many United Methodist congregations may be fueling pessimism about the potential for future salary growth.

There are also young clergy who are not at all interested in ladder climbing, even if there is one. They want to be able to do the kind of ministry that they believe is vital for the church and the world; and the current ways of setting salaries and making appointments make it unlikely they can afford to stay in those kinds of ministries and support their families for the long term.

For example, some young clergy understand themselves to be called to urban ministry, and they have worked to develop their knowledge and skills so that they can serve urban congregations faithfully and fruitfully among persons who are homeless or marginalized in other ways. Funding for such mission ventures tends to be from denominational funds and for a limited period. Therefore, in order to continue this form of ministry, some discover they must also become fund-raising entrepreneurs, something for which they are not trained. For some young clergy, this situation leads to disillusionment with the larger church and its leaders. The loss of financial support, without help in developing new competencies that they may need to continue such ministry, becomes a symbol for what they experience as a lack of commitment to mission by the church as a whole.

Salary concerns for clergy of all ages are unlikely to go away, particularly in this era of heightened budgetary pressure. There is no magic wand to wave to make it better. But we believe that honest and open dialogue about financial concerns, greater attention to differing financial situations among clergy, and more innovative and flexible attitudes toward clergy compensation will go a long way toward satisfying the salary concerns of young clergy.

CHAPTER TEN

The Challenge of Educational Debt

All resources of the church—educational, institutional, theological, financial—need to be brought to bear to avoid the gathering storm of debt that threatens the next generation of clergy and lay church professionals.
Anthony Ruger

Seminary tuition and the level of educational debt incurred by students have both increased dramatically in recent decades. With denominational support as a percentage of the cost of theological education declining, a greater proportion of costs has shifted to students preparing for ministry. In the 1930s, for example, denominations paid 90 percent of the seminary cost of educating future pastors. In 1968, the figure in the United Methodist Church was 32 percent. By 1990, the denomination contributed only 20 percent of the cost of educating each student. Today it is even less, and it appears that the percentage will continue to decrease in coming years.

The percentage of Master of Divinity graduates in North America who borrow for their seminary education has increased significantly in recent decades, as has the percentage who are borrowing at high levels. In fact, the average amounts borrowed almost doubled between 1991 and 2001, even after accounting for inflation.[1] Each year, more and more United Methodist seminary graduates enter ministry with higher levels of educational debt from seminary and, in some cases, from college. If this trend is not reversed, aspiring clergy with limited personal financial resources will face significant difficulties.

Young clergy are particularly vulnerable to the risks associated with mounting educational debt. Although increasing debt is a burden for seminarians of all ages, younger students who enter seminary immediately after college, or within a year or two of graduating, have had less opportunity than older students to pay down college loans. They are, therefore, at greater risk for amassing larger cumulative debt that includes both college and seminary loans.

The Lewis Center's survey of young United Methodist elders found that 63 percent report entering ministry with educational debt requiring years to repay; and 12 percent say they have missed an educational loan payment because they did not have the money. Fifteen percent of the survey respondents reported seminary debts of $30,000 or more; 37 percent had seminary debts between $10,000 and $30,000; and 17 percent had debts of $10,000 or less. In addition to this, 5 percent had college debts of more than $30,000; 31 percent had college debts of between $10,000 and $30,000; and 20 percent had college debt of $10,000 or less.

The burden of large educational debt is compounded by the fact that young pastors traditionally have very low starting salaries. One young United Methodist pastor put it quite bluntly, "My salary is $30,000, and my student loan debt is $60,000." Younger students are less likely than their older classmates to have accumulated assets, to own a home, or to have a spouse who earns a high income. And with increasing educational costs, the next generation of young leaders who have yet to enter seminary will face an even more serious challenge.

The United Methodist Church has a strong tradition of generous support for theological education, but competing claims and financial strains have led to a smaller proportionate investment in the cost of educating seminary students. Since 1968, the Ministerial Education Fund (MEF) has been the denomination's primary vehicle for funding seminary education. Seventy-five percent of MEF funds are used to underwrite theological education at the thirteen United Methodist seminaries, including the Course of Study Program and Division of Ordained Ministry programs. The remaining 25 percent remains in each annual conference to be used for scholarships and other clergy education needs. Local churches, conference boards of ordained ministry, clergy, laity, and seminaries all have a stake in this innovative fund that is the envy of other denominations.

The central feature of the original plan, modeled after a jurisdictional "Two Percent Fund," was to set aside two percent of church expenditures for the education of future pastors and church leaders. The genius of this formula was that money for future leadership rose with overall church expenditures. This worked well until local church expenditures started growing so rapidly that there was pressure to change the formula. While the two percent concept was retained, the base on which it is calculated has changed. The base is no longer all church expenditures. The pattern in recent times has been to adjust the base to produce a predetermined sum, rather than allowing the contributions for the MEF to grow in proportion to other expenditures. The effect of these changes has been to limit the growth of the fund and diminish the proportion of seminary costs provided by the denomination.

Increasing Seminary Debt

Seminary debt trends are clearly documented by research conducted by Anthony Ruger and his colleagues at the Center for the Study of Theological Education at Auburn Theological Seminary in New York. Their most recent report, *The Gathering Storm: The Educational Debt of Theological Students* published in 2005, tracks changes in student debt between 1991 and 2001. It concluded that both the extent and level of educational borrowing had grown steadily during that decade.[2] In 1991, 47 percent of Master of Divinity graduates borrowed for their seminary education; in 2001, 63 percent of M.Div. graduates had borrowed. The change in the percentage of students borrowing at high levels is even more dramatic. In 1991, only 1 percent had borrowed $30,000 or more, while 21 percent of the graduates in 2001 had borrowed at that level.[3] The average amounts borrowed almost doubled in the ten years after accounting for inflation.[4]

During this same period, the level of educational debt seminarians were carrying from their undergraduate studies also increased significantly. But their undergraduate debts were less than those of college students overall. One explanation offered for the difference was the high percentage of seminary students who were over 30 and had presumably had enough time to retire undergraduate debts. When seminaries are successful in recruiting younger students, the authors warn, "They will likely be confronted with students entering with considerable debt."[5]

How do United Methodist students fit into these broad trends? In research commissioned by the Lewis Center for this book on younger clergy, Anthony Ruger compared the student debt of United Methodist seminary graduates in 2001 to the overall average for seminary graduates that year. He found that a higher percentage of United Methodists borrow for their seminary education—70 percent of all United Methodist 2001 graduates had borrowed, compared to 63 percent of all 2001 seminary grads. Of those United Methodists who borrow, the size of their loans generally follows the pattern of other seminarians. Of the United Methodist graduates in 2001, 18 percent had borrowed less than $10,000; 30 percent had borrowed between $10,000 and $30,000; and 22 percent had borrowed more than $30,000. Among those who borrowed, the average borrowed for all educational expenses for United Methodists was about 8 percent higher than for all seminary graduates in 2001—$33,858 compared to $31,376.

The picture is more complex when one explores differences among United Methodist seminary graduates, according to Ruger's research. Gender makes a difference in how much money is borrowed. Counting everyone, including those with *no* debt, the average borrowed by women for education was 31 percent higher than for men—$28,265 for women versus $21,555 for men. Looking only at those *with* debt, the average borrowed by women for education in 2001 was 21 percent higher than for men—$37,280 for women versus $30,697 for men. Marital status is also a relevant variable related to debt. Among United Methodist graduates in 2001, average educational debt was lowest among married men ($21,710), followed by married women ($24,517), and then single men ($26,460). Single women had the highest debt ($31,205).

Young Clergy Debt

Ruger's analysis found that the average educational debt for 2001 United Methodist seminary graduates who were 30 or younger was about 90 percent that of United Methodist graduates over 30. Women under 30 have average educational debt 29 percent higher than men under 30—$26,241 compared to $20,281 for men—about the same percentage difference that occurs between women and men over 30.

In addition, the 2007 Lewis Center survey questioned young clergy (under 35) about educational debt and other financial matters. Since many of the respondents have been out of seminary for several years, one would expect to find evidence of some debts being paid down or retired, and indeed, the survey's findings seem consistent with this expectation. Comparing the Lewis Center's findings with what Ruger learned about United Methodist seminary graduates in 2001, one finds that the percentage of young elders and deacons reporting no remaining seminary debt is about the same—around 30 percent. There is a decrease in the percentage owing over $30,000 and an increase in those owing between $10,000 and $30,000. This shift is presumably a result of the paying down of debt.

Debt Figures for United Methodist Clergy

	2001 U.M. Seminary Graduates	**Under-35 Elders and Deacons Responding to Lewis Center Survey**
No Seminary Debt	30%	31%
Debt Under $10,000	18%	17%
Debt Between $10,001 and $29,999	30%	37%
Debt of $30,000 or More	22%	15%

Implications and Recommendations

The 2005 report, *The Gathering Storm: The Educational Debt of Theological Students*, concludes by saying that if the trend toward increasing seminary debts continues unabated, "the consequences would be severe."[6] Seminary training for clergy will become increasingly available only to those of means or to those who become impoverished in the process. It will become increasingly difficult for clergy with high levels of debt to serve in smaller congregations or in new ministries with few resources because of the imperative to earn enough money to repay debts. A concerted effort is required by all involved to address this increasing dilemma.

Seminaries must continue their efforts at raising funds for financial assistance. In most seminaries, funds for financial aid grants have increased dramatically in recent years, but the needs are still great. Financial planning is becoming an increasingly important part of a seminary's role in working with students. Seminaries can help students who may be thinking about only one semester at a time to examine their financial situation comprehensively and develop realistic plans for repayment of loans.

Summary of Facts about Educational Debt

• Over the past century the cost of educating future clergy has been shifting from denominations to students.

• Between 1991 and 2001, the extent and level of indebtedness of North American seminary graduates grew rapidly. The percentage who borrowed increased from 47 percent to 63 percent. The percentage borrowing more than $30,000 rose from 1 percent to 21 percent. And the average amount borrowed doubled, even after accounting for inflation.

• Undergraduate debt borne by seminarians also increased significantly from 1991 to 2001, although it is below the overall average for college graduates, perhaps because such a high proportion of seminary students are over 30.

• The percentage of 2001 United Methodist seminary graduates who borrowed was above the norm for all seminary graduates—70 percent compared to 63 percent.

• Among those who borrowed, United Methodist 2001 graduates had total educational debts that were 8 percent above the average for 2001 seminary graduates—$33,858 compared to $31,376.

• Average educational borrowing is higher for United Methodist women than men. Single students also borrow more than married students. Single female graduates had the highest average educational debt among 2001 graduates—44 percent higher than married men.

• Young United Methodist seminary graduates generally have debt that is about 90 percent that of over-30 graduates. Among young graduates, it still holds true that women's debt is about 30 percent higher than that of men.

• More than half of young United Methodist clergy have educational debts of $10,000 or more. Of those who graduated in 2001, 22 percent had debts of more than $30,000.

They can also encourage students to seek actively educational funds from multiple sources, and inform students of the vast array of possible income sources. For example, information on the scholarship resources available through the General Board of Higher Education and Ministry (GBHEM) and the United Methodist Higher Education Foundation (UMHEF) should be provided to each candidate by both the conference and seminaries. The Office of Loans and Scholarships of the GBHEM does a splendid job of providing funds that are entrusted to them to those who have need and match the intentions of the donors. The Double Your Dollars scholarship program that was begun in recent years by the UMHEF has been a marvelous means of helping congregations to maximize the benefit of funds that they contribute for students attending United Methodist institutions.

Likewise, districts and conferences that want to be supportive can ask students about their educational funding and debt repayment plans, and use all available conference resources to help seminary students get their basic education. In some conferences, foundations are a generous source of educational funds. Some conference foundations also assist entering clergy with financial planning, and a few will provide grants to assist clergy in particularly difficult financial situations because of educational debt.

Congregations are called to pray for those they nurture and send to seminary, and they also need to provide financial assistance. Seminary students are sometimes reluctant to ask their congregations or groups within their home churches for help. Pastors and staff-parish relations committees can be advocates for those they have affirmed and recommended for ordained ministry, arranging a time each year for the seminarian to speak to the congregation and finding ways to direct funds toward the student's education. Even congregations that do not have one of their own members in seminary can develop a sense of mission by assisting in the education and development of young clergy. Establishing endowed scholarships at seminaries and within congregations—often to honor a beloved pastor—can provide an ongoing fund from which students can be helped.

First United Methodist Church in Montgomery, Alabama, has set a wonderful example of what a congregation can do for young clergy. Their recently retired pastor, Dr. Karl Stegall, first became aware of the financial needs of seminarians as a district superintendent working with many student local pastors. Believing that the church had a responsibility to support those starting out in ministry, he initiated a Seminary Scholarship Fund when he came to First Church. He recruited seminary student sponsors who would contribute $1,200 a year for three years for a seminary student. The sponsors and students came to know each other. Over 200 seminary students from the Alabama-West Florida Conference have benefited from these sponsors over the past 23 years. In 2006, as Dr. Stegall was approaching retirement, several church members approached him about creating an endowment for the fund that would become the Karl K. Stegall Seminary Scholarship Fund. Currently, they have raised over $1.65 million dollars for this fund, which is a testimony to Dr. Stegall's inspired vision of engaging laity in the active support of those who will be the future leaders of their churches.

Modest salaries will probably always be a fact of life for young clergypersons. But severe financial hardship, or even potential bankruptcy, need not be. One of the most important things that congregations and denominational leaders can do to lighten the load for future young leaders is to fund more adequately the cost of theological education. Supporting seminaries in their efforts to keep tuition affordable is important to making the pathway to ministry accessible to all, as is scholarship assistance for those most in need.

CHAPTER ELEVEN

Bridging the Generation Gap

The paradox of aging is that every generation perceives itself as justifiably different from its predecessor, but plans as if its successor generation will be the same.[1]
Charles Handy

Perhaps it is inevitable that each generation looks at other generations with some degree of suspicion and stereotypes. Younger people tend to view established leaders as workaholics or pure pragmatists, too attached to the trappings of success and position, shallow thinkers only interested in the mechanics of the church, and intolerant of different views. At the same time, established leaders will see those younger as too emotional, impulsive, impatient, unwilling to work hard and pay their dues, wanting everything too fast, holding unrealistic expectations, and having no respect for authority and customs.

For today's young clergy, however, normal intergenerational difficulties are magnified by the growing age gap between them and their congregations and clergy colleagues. Because the median age of elders and church members has risen dramatically, young clergy *seem* younger and more different in relation to their congregations and other clergy than have young pastors in previous generations. Young clergy also feel intergenerational tension more intensely because there are fewer of them.

Over 80 percent of the young elders responding to the Lewis Center's 2007 survey said that their congregations were open to receiving a young pastor. Yet this relatively simple statement belies the sense of a generational gap that comes across clearly in some of their stories. "Older members of the congregation don't always take you seriously," said one young pastor. "They say 'you have a lot to learn' and then pat you on the head." Another said, "Most of our congregation are older than us and think we don't know what we are talking about." Indeed, 58 percent of young elders responding to the Lewis Center's survey agreed or strongly agreed with the statement: "I often feel disrespected because of my age."

Differing values and competing mind-sets are sometimes a part of the problem. "Everybody is not on the same page," said one. "The way I view things that are important and urgent may or may not be the same for the congregation I am serving." Unfortunately, these differences reinforce the sense that some young clergy have of being unwelcome or disrespected. "New ideas and different ways of doing things are not appreciated or valued. We are dismissed as 'idealistic' or a 'weird liberal.' "

Young clergy who are in tune with the culture and mores of their own generation often speak a different language than the older people in the church. "'Post-modern' and 'pop culture' are languages that I speak fluently," says one young clergy. "This means I experience a language barrier with the greater Church because its language reflects a whole different era than I've ever known . . . [When I use my] language in sermons and in the context of everyday ministry, the response is usually glazed-eyes and judgment of 'that must be a young person thing.' "[2] Another young clergy serving in North Carolina says he was ridiculed for using pop cultural references in sermons.

One young pastor put it this way: "It is as if we are speaking a parallel language, we use the same words but mean totally different things. . . . Words like 'discipleship,' 'faithfulness' and 'mission' seem to have different meanings depending on the age of the congregant. Trying to move gracefully between our older members and the precarious few younger people who come in seeking a faith-journey becomes a careful balancing act. Most of the time it is as if we are pastoring two congregations, speaking two languages, and hoping that as the older congregation dies out a younger congregation will come forward, ready to take the lead in a new kind of church."[3]

Young clergy whose native tongue is postmodern are pressured to change their accents to accommodate the church culture, says Brian McLaren, a leading voice in the emergent church conversation. "But to the degree they do," McLaren says, "they lose their ability to communicate with their own generation. This is an agonizing dilemma."[4]

Young clergy can also feel caught between two worlds when interacting with older clergy colleagues. As token young adults and Gen Xers, many young clergy are asked to participate in conference committees and boards. One young clergy, in a conference where more than half the elders are now retired, serves on five different conference committees and fears burnout.[5] Sometimes older colleagues are all too eager to hand off burdensome committee chores to newcomers, but unwilling to listen to new ideas. And while young clergy may be doing lots of committee work, they are quick to observe the virtual exclusion of younger clergy from more significant leadership roles, including General and Jurisdictional Conference representatives.

"Conference committees, firmly entrenched in their conference status and structure, look to us for ideas and input that they probably do not want to hear. We try diplomatically to offer our perspective on the subject at hand, knowing that very little of the conference business has any relevance for members of our generation. Yet again, we feel torn between the church that we love and the perceived reality that its structures and programs are, to be diplomatic, not helpful."[6]

"This is the problem," one southeastern clergyman wrote. "No one listens." Recalling one clergy committee gathering, he said that the older members of the committee asked him, "What do younger people think about this?" Replying that he could not speak for all people his age, he gave his best assessment of what he thought the committee would hear if talking to a representative group of the younger persons. The response from the committee members was, "That's not what young people think." They simply dismissed and ignored his opinion, despite the fact that it was, in all likelihood, better informed than their own.

The Lewis Center survey asked young clergy, "What one thing could your annual conference do to be more supportive of young clergy?" Issues having to do with appointments and financial support were mentioned most frequently. But a large number of the suggestions involved requests to be taken seriously, to treat young clergy with more respect, and to give them more leadership in conference affairs. Several specific suggestions capture the mood of some young clergy: "Don't look down on us because we are young. Don't patronize us either." "Respect us and stop treating us like little kids." "Quit acting like I couldn't possibly be effective just because I look like your children, grandchildren, or youth group."

Suggestions for Established Clergy and Denominational Leaders

Given such inevitable generation gaps, who is responsible for first reaching out to bridge such distances? It is incumbent upon those who are older to reach out. Those who are younger are not nearly as likely to feel they are in a position to initiate dialogue. A function of leadership is to serve as a listener and interpreter among the generations, helping each to understand the views of the others.[7]

Conversations occurring only within generations will normally center on whether we are going to have to change to accommodate *them* or whether *they* are going to shape up and see things *our* way. The hand of invitation must first be extended by current leaders to the leaders of tomorrow. If the established leaders reach out with authenticity, care, humility, and a willingness to learn, then emerging leaders will respond enthusiastically and reciprocally. "They will be willing to let go of their cynical suspicions and some of the impulsivity that accompanies their impatience, to gain the great benefits of learning alongside those who have come before them," according to those who help secular leaders bridge generations in the workplace.[8]

Henri Nouwen reminds us that the word *generosity* includes the term *gen*, which we also find in such words as *generation*. This term, from the Latin *genus* and the Greek *genos*, refers to our being of one kind. Generosity is a giving that comes from the knowledge of the intimate bond that already exists.[9] This bond means that we enter conversations knowing we have much in common.

Work by Jennifer Deal finds that people from different generations are far more alike than different in their views, values, hopes, and dreams. Deal found that, while there are a few differences, the primary values that people hold are remarkably consistent across generations. If this is the case, why the perennial conflict among generations? Although basic values may be the same, how various generations express those values tends to differ greatly. An example occurs when young people dress casually and older people view that as a sign of disrespect—but the young people are not expressing disrespect, they just want to dress casually. What is often seen as a conflict of values is more likely to be about *how* people express their values rather than the values themselves.[10]

It is clear that all generations share a desire for respect. Each generation has an image of what respect means and when such respect is missing. Deal's work finds that *where* one stands changes what is understood as respect. Older generations tend to interpret *respect* to mean that deference is given to their greater experience and wisdom. However, younger generations have no expectations that people will defer to them. Instead, younger persons feel respected when their views are sought and their ideas are taken seriously. Therefore, listening becomes a key part of being established leaders. It is important for such leaders to remember that questions are not a sign of disrespect.[11]

Listening could be the most effective thing that conference leaders and other established clergy could do to make their conferences and other church venues more attractive and hospitable for younger clergy. Listening is simple and easy to do, but it will not happen unless there is planning. One encouraging sign in many conferences is that bishops, superintendents, conference staff, and others are initiating regular conversations with younger clergy. It is crucial to remember that for younger people, respect comes from being heard and taken seriously. No effort will yield greater rewards for the time expended. Established leaders must take heed: listen, listen, listen.

Trust Is Essential

Establishing and maintaining a high level of trust is key to generational cooperation. Credibility is the foundation upon which all effective work is built. An established leader wins trust slowly. The young will give established leaders a degree of deference because of position. However, the credibility needed for partnership in ministry must be worked out among people.

There are three building blocks for establishing trust and credibility across generations. *Relationships* are primary. Every encounter with another person serves to enhance or decrease trust. There is no better way to build credibility than by spending time with other persons, getting to know them, and giving them a chance to get to know you. Another element is *character*. Every time another person sees consistency between words and actions, respect grows. Knowing that another person has the highest integrity adds to trust. The third element is *competence*. In addition to good personal relationships and demonstrated character, established leaders must also be seen as competent in helping address the important challenges being faced. When young leaders see these three factors present in established leaders over a period of time a sense of trust develops that makes common mission possible.[12]

Common Mission as a Generational Bridge

If there is a leadership vacuum, the natural tendency will be for all generations to view whatever happens in the church through their generational lens. The challenge for established leaders is to reframe the discussion around a compelling common purpose. Then everyone is challenged to view their distinct generational strengths through the lens of the common mission. From this new perspective, the differences among generations that once seemed a liability now appear as an abundance of diversity that can be brought to the task of implementing the common goal.

This provides a means for persons across generations to gather around the task and thus live their way into a new understanding of each other as they work together. It permits us to form relationships that respectfully leverage the differences each generation brings. Extraordinary things can be done when people work side by side to pursue what all consider to be God's vision for them.

Suggestions for Churches Receiving a Young Pastor

Churches that receive a young pastor should first remember how lucky they are. Many congregations say they want a younger pastor, but few have the opportunity. They should not, however, assume their church will automatically reach younger people just because of the age of the pastor. Having a young pastor might improve the likelihood of a congregation connecting with young people, but not without openness to other kinds of change. Congregations sincere in their desire to work with a younger pastor to reach emerging generations must be flexible and open to new ideas and possibilities.

Congregrants are encouraged to treat a young clergyperson as a pastor, not as they would their children or grandchildren. It can be helpful to consider how one regards other young professionals. A patient being treated by a young doctor, for example, may not be able to help thinking to himself or herself, "That doctor is young enough to be my child or grandchild." But that kind of thinking is quickly set aside in deference to the doctor's professional role. In the end, many older people find themselves reassured when dealing with a young professional who has the benefit of more recent training. This is the same kind of regard the congregation can offer to a young pastor.

How Established Church Leaders Can Relate Better to Younger Clergy

- Demonstrate interest, care, and responsiveness to concerns.
- Do not act as if people owe you trust, but extend trust to others before it is earned.
- Since undue meaning is often read into your words and deeds, pay close attention to your words and actions to make sure they are consistent with what you want to convey.
- Get in touch with your need for control.
- Ask probing, thoughtful questions, then take the time to listen carefully and remember the answers. Never ask for input that you do not want or will not consider. Always complete the communication loop by getting back to people to report what has happened.
- Avoid being defensive when challenged. Demonstrate that people can ask you hard questions without your being resentful or retaliating.
- Conduct meetings that maximize participation and that limit presentations.
- Talk about your dreams and learn the dreams of others and how you can help realize them.
- Be clear about expectations.
- Make sure people have what they need to be successful. Ask what they need from you.
- Demonstrate competence, and always do what you say you are going to do.

• Talk about how decisions will be made and what their part is or is not and why. Once decisions are made tell people and give reasons why.

• Show respect and recognition for good work and celebrate victories.

• Remember that you probably have income and perks that the younger clergy do not have, so do not make a big deal about things you may have or do that are out of their reach.

• Do share privileges such as meals, books, and attendance at events that are available to you.

• Share information generously.

• Do not complain about the hard work or difficulties that go with your position.

• Show you can be in the background with grace.

• Look out for the best interests of younger persons when you have the opportunity. Show an interest in their compensation.

• Do not knowingly mislead. If you cannot tell the truth, say you cannot talk about the subject.

• Help the young learn and grow. Everyone wants to develop and improve.

Church members can also take time to remember what it was like to be young or to be responsible for a young family. Then they may not be too quick to criticize a young pastor who struggles with the number of night meetings on the calendar. Expecting around the clock availability from a pastor is unreasonable, regardless of his or her age.

Younger and older generations in the church would do well to keep in mind the notion, "We're all in this together." Especially within the community of faith, what unites us in Christ is far greater than what divdes us as representatives of one generation or another. We are called in "all humility and gentleness, with patience, bearing with one another in love, and making every effort to maintain the unity of the Spirit" (Ephesians 4:2-3 NRSV).

CHAPTER TWELVE

The Church Must Change

It is not that young adults have changed but that the church has not.
Matt Miofsky, young pastor, Missouri

The United Methodist Church is suffering today the effects of our church having been in decline for more than a generation. The last year that The United Methodist Church showed a membership gain was 1964 (Methodist and Evangelical United Brethren combined). That was the year the first of the baby boomers graduated from high school and the last of the baby boomers were born. In other words, it was a long time ago. Clergy who entered ordained ministry after 1964 have never been a part of a growing denomination, and many, if not most, have spent the majority of their years in ministry serving churches that believe their best years were in the past.

In addition to all that our church, or any church, is, we are also an organization. And the church does not receive "a religious exemption" from many of the patterns of other organizations. The study of leadership has shown us that in declining organizations, there is a failure to attract sufficient quality leadership. The leadership base of declining organizations grows smaller and smaller. So just at the time when the organization needs its best leaders in greatest numbers, the pool of quality leadership tends to be smallest.

The issue of the quality and number of young people entering ordained ministry must be seen side by side with the quality and vitality of the church itself. The church's overall health is the most important factor determining who comes into ordained ministry. Some say that organizations tend to get the leadership they deserve, not the leadership they need, but any questions or concerns about the quality of leadership must be directed at the church itself. For example, why does the church in this particular era allow so many to ignore the call of God? Has there been a shift in who responds and who does not? Yes. We have already seen the dramatic decline in the number of young clergy. At the same time there is evidence that the quality of new clergy of all ages may not be what it was in some past times. While he was dean of Harvard Divinity School, Ronald F. Thiemann reported on a study conducted by the American Medical Association in 1851. They recorded the careers chosen by 12,400 men who graduated from eight leading colleges between 1800 and 1850. The largest group, 26 percent, went into ordained ministry, followed by 25 percent who went into law, and 8 percent who became physicians. If such a survey of comparable colleges were done today, ministry would not rank high enough to be included in the statistics.[1]

This concern is not new. "Fewer and fewer undergraduate students who graduated at the top of their classes are coming to theological schools," observed theologian Schubert Ogden nearly 15 years ago. "They are going on to other professions and careers. This is the problem of a church that is not reproducing the bulk of its leadership from the highest ranks of its young persons."[2] Also several years ago, *Newsweek* magazine quoted Robert W. Lynn, a noted observer of American religion, as saying that neither the Christian nor Jewish traditions are attracting sufficient leaders of quality and that many laity are therefore "bored out of their minds."[3]

Leander Keck links the enlistment dilemma directly to the condition of the church itself. "The impression is abroad," he contends, "that the church does not welcome strength since it is more a place to find a support group than a channel for energy and talent, more a place where the bruised find solace than where the strong find companions and challenge."[4]

While improvements in enlistment, seminary education, and board of ordained ministry processes are necessary, these things are not what keep people from entering the ministry. Most people never get that far. A young former United Methodist pastor believes that it is a mistake to assume that there are few young clergy because no one invited them. "This approach would ignore a significant element in the equation—the church itself." So, our efforts for younger clergy are tied inextricably to the renewal and revitalization of the church.

The Aging of a Historically Young Denomination

Early American Methodists could have focused only on the needs of existing adult members. They chose instead to give attention to the future and to the young. Their passion for establishing colleges is a prime example. Historian Nathan Hatch reminds us that Methodists were virtually alone among the American denominations in the extent of their educational emphasis. For most of the nineteenth century, Methodists founded one or more colleges or universities each year. Indeed, over a thousand educational institutions were founded, although many did not survive.

Various youth and young adult organizations and movements played key roles in the development of vigorous leadership for the church. The Sunday school movement, for example, was a major effort toward the evangelism and education of a new generation of Christians. The Sunday school movement was not a strictly Methodist endeavor, but Methodists contributed significantly to its leadership and benefited greatly from its success.

Today's Situation—a Rapidly Aging Church

The percentage of church members aged 50 and above has continued to grow for a number of decades now. Persons of this age constitute a higher percentage of church members than of the population as a whole. This is true even when people too young to be church members are excluded from the comparison. "I genuinely care and fear as I visit churches and see them frequented largely by older people," writes Walter Brueggemann. "It is like visiting Wilder's *Our Town* in a season of despair a generation later."[5] The United Methodist Church within the United States, like the other mainline churches, is an aging church.

One unfortunate reason the aging of the denomination has not received more attention is that in declining churches, especially those with aging congregations, the availability of financial resources tends to continue, and perhaps even increase. But in growing churches, needs run ahead of money by two or three years as newer, often younger, members join. At first, the newer members may not bring the same resources and commitment as more established members. The opposite is the case in aging congregations. Overall, people have more assets after age 50 than at any other time in their lives. Although membership in The United Methodist Church began to decline in the mid-1960s, a financial decline was not felt immediately—because of inflation and because the aging members who remained had more resources. One can only imagine what would have happened if membership and money trends over the last forty years had been reversed.

The next two decades will bring the death of a large group of United Methodists who were nurtured, in another era, with an exemplary level of dedication and commitment. Their millions of dollars in financial assets that have kept the church afloat during the past forty years of decline will also be gone, for the most part. Just as important, this generation's energy, passion, and sacrifice will be lost. Their blessed memory and fine example will continue to inspire the church. Some will continue to give to the church in their name through estate plans. But in the final analysis, churches cannot thrive on either inherited faithfulness or inherited money. There must be a vision and enthusiasm to capture the hearts and souls of a new generation of disciples.

United Methodist pastor Don Haynes makes an uncomfortable point humorous. He says every United Methodist leader should thank God every night for medical science. Without the advances in medicine and longer life expectancy, The United Methodist Church would have already died. Humor usually requires some degree of overstatement. So it is in this case, but not by much. Because the average age of United Methodists is higher than the national average, the death rate each year for United Methodists is higher than in the general population. This trend will continue to get worse every year so long as the average age in the church is increasing.

There is another factor contributing to the aging of our church. The birthrates among the traditional constituencies of mainline churches are the lowest of any denominational family in the United States. Birthrates are so low that even if every child of the current members of mainline denominations joined their family's church, there still would not be growth.[6]

The Church Must Change—An Outwardly Focused Church

Respondents to the Lewis Center's survey of young clergy said that a "desire to make a difference in the life of the church" was one of the top factors in discerning their call, but a "desire to preserve the traditions of the church" was one of the lowest rated factors. "Ministers are weary of the caretaking and management functions that are assigned in the modern church," says Rebecca Chopp.[7] However, in declining organizations, inordinate attention is given to these caretaking functions because good administration and management can cause a declining organization to appear healthy for many years after the power has gone. Good caretakers will preserve the forms that developed in a previous vital era even after the power and vitality from that era have disappeared, giving the illusion that everything is still the way it used to be. However, such caretaking has no power to attract the most gifted people who seek to be leaders around a new vision appropriate for a new day. The aspects of ministry that young clergy report as most draining are administration, conflict resolution, and meetings.

Churches, along with other organizations in decline, seem to think that the right leader can develop a plan to reach out to others to join the enterprise. But existing members never seem to think that the church itself will need to change its ways to reach others. While there needs to be good leadership and a plan to reach out to others, success will depend at least as much on changes made internally as on what the church is doing to reach people externally. So it is with denominational life. Young clergy want to be a part of shaping a future, but that future will need to be different from the near past in some significant ways. One of those ways is a shift from an inwardly focused church to an outwardly focused church.

For young clergy, ministry begins with meeting people's needs, both spiritual and material. Congregations exist to serve people, not the other way around. This concern for people links young clergy with their generational cohorts outside the church who seem to care little about organized religion. A deep concern for the plight of people and a desire to help people should be a common bond for a new generation and the link that binds the church with those outside the church who are deeply concerned about helping others.

Leadership in the Wesleyan spirit begins with people, not congregations. The pressure to survive has caused many churches to forget the mission for which they were established in the first place. The message that comes through in the church often is not one of serving those most in need, but asking people to maintain the church. Young clergy are not excited about asking people "to do something for the church." They are willing to serve people, and to give others an opportunity to serve in the name of Christ to meet the needs of a hurting world. The Wesleyan movement began not for itself but for others. Thriving and serving were indeed linked. The growth of the Wesleyan enterprise is directly related to its identification with the needs of all God's children.[8]

The Church Must Change—A Growing Church

Young clergy today may be few in numbers, but they have an abundance of commitment. "For a young person to become a United Methodist pastor today," one young clergy said, "we must have had a very strong call." They know themselves, in the words of Paul recorded in Ephesians, as being "made a minister, according to the gift of God's grace." They also know that such ministers are granted the privilege of proclaiming the good news of "the unfathomable riches of Christ" (Ephesians 3:7, 8 NASB). If their message is good news, then it follows that it is imperative that such a message be shared with others.

Many churches demonstrate little sense of responsibility or accountability for the number of lives left untouched in their communities. Young clergy know this. They sometimes resent being criticized by clergy who have overseen the decline of the denomination. They are not interested in blaming those who are older, but neither are they interested in continuing to go in a failed direction. They want to join with others—young and old, clergy and lay—to help chart a new course that leads toward growth rather than accepting decline as normal.

In a society where the population is growing and getting younger and more diverse, it is not likely that a church will attract large numbers of capable young leaders until it demonstrates that it can reach more people, younger people, and more diverse people. The aging of the church works against all three of these goals. The death rate of an aging church is higher, the average age is older, and people of color in the population are disproportionately younger. An aging church is unlikely to become larger and more diverse, while a younger church is likely to be growing and becoming more diverse. Three questions that United Methodists would do well to keep in mind if the United Methodist witness is to strengthen in the years ahead:

Are we reaching more people for Christ?
Are we reaching younger people for Christ?
Are we reaching diverse people for Christ?

The Church Must Change—A More Broadly Inclusive Church

The emerging generation is known for being more tolerant than older generations. Time will tell if the tolerance of their youth is maintained, but it is safe to say that many prejudices that have shaped church life in the past will not be tolerated by new generations. They have grown up with far more diversity than previous generations. Their contemporaries reflect more differences in race, language, nationality, and family circumstances than do the peers of their parents. Diversity is a way of life for them. Observing the sharp contrast between their diverse world and the homogenous world of the church, some young clergy fear that the church is not only failing to reach out to their contemporaries, but may actually be alienating the very persons they seek to recruit for ordained ministry.

Diversity of People

The Wesleyan movement began by including those who were different socially and economically. Wesley sought a church open to those who felt rejected by society and God. Early American Methodists were multicultural. But American Methodism's record is a mixed one with many backward steps and chapters that bring shame today. The Wesleyan spirit of inclusiveness soon gave way to the pressure of social convention in America. It has taken generations and will take many more to undo the damage to the soul of the church. Still the Wesleyan spirit at its best can continue to inform leadership today.

The need for a church inclusive of all people is paramount today. A church known for exclusiveness has little future among the young. The growing racial and ethnic diversity of the United States will shape the future of all institutions in ways hard to imagine. The church's appeal to the young, including young clergy, will be shaped largely by its willingness and ability to respond to the changing face of America.

Future young clergy must include gifted persons from many racial, ethnic, and national backgrounds. United Methodist seminaries have led the way in attracting diverse student bodies. However, if the respondents to the Lewis Center's 2007 young clergy survey are an indication, little progress has been made toward diversity. Ninety-six percent of young United Methodist elders participating in that survey were white.

Diversity of Thought

Wesley sought to hold different, and often competing, claims together with integrity. He did so because he felt a kinship with many different people and perspectives. He saw much to value in traditions not his own. Thus, Wesley's approach bridged many divisions within Christian thought and practice. Too often churches have not sought to bridge such gaps. Indeed, well-meaning Christians have sometimes been the source of greater division and distrust. While desiring to include others, some of our practices make others feel unwelcome.

Perhaps one reason many young clergy are taken with the emergent church conversation is that it provides a safe zone to discuss issues of faith in terms other than the traditional left and right categories. For example, a clergywoman with no evangelical theological background, upon reading a book about the emergent church by an evangelical writer, said, "This is the first book I've read that understands my generation." Repeatedly we have seen persons coming from different theological backgrounds finding excitement rather than argument through emergent conversations.

Does this mean young clergy are not committed to theology and issues? That is far from the truth. Many young clergy, though not all, are open to a broader inclusiveness of ideas. They are much less likely to be turned off by and less likely to exclude other clergy who do not share their theology or politics. They also know that concern for poverty, justice, war, and racism are not the prerogative of any one theological perspective. They know from experience and study that theological categories often do not predict how effective clergy will be in leading social change. We need to remember that the Wesleyan movement did not begin as a doctrinal debate.

Another dimension must be noted. While it is true that most young clergy seem to demonstrate a tolerance that permits them to be open to those with different views, a significant minority come at things quite differently. A common phrase for the first group is, "I believe we should begin to live out our commitment to open hearts, open minds, open doors." The second group would more likely say, "No wonder we are declining. We no longer stand for anything. We need to be clear about our standards and make no exceptions."

The whole church is faced with the challenge of entering the zone where it is safe to be different, even in challenging some conventional wisdom and practice. But diverse people with diverse ideas must hold something in common that is stronger than all their differences. The goal of inclusion is unity of purpose and direction without forcing uniformity. Inclusion for people of faith requires a common center, despite countless differences. And, for the people called Methodist, that center has always been Jesus Christ.

CHAPTER THIRTEEN

Summary and Recommendations

The young clergy crisis is a complex and multifaceted problem that does not lend itself to simple responses or quick fixes. We encourage church leaders to focus their attention on the problem, to enter into dialogue and study on the relevant issues, and consider the actions that can be taken within the context of their areas of responsibility. Concerted effort by leaders at every level of the church will be required to increase the number of young persons entering ordained ministry, and to ensure that our church has the leadership needed to reach emerging generations for Christ.

Summary of Findings

Young clergy matter. While persons of *all* ages bring vital gifts to the practice of ministry, there are important reasons why the pool of clergy must include a proportionate number of younger persons. In addition to the energy and creativity normally associated with youthfulness, research shows that younger clergy are more successful as church planters. They often are more able to connect with other young persons. And they can devote a lifetime to serving the church and honing their ministry skills.

There has been a serious and sustained decline in the number and percentage of young clergy. The percentage of United Methodist elders under the age of 35 in the United States was less than 5 percent in 2007, having declined from over 15 percent in 1985 and over 20 percent in the early 1970s. Many other denominations report similarly low percentages of young clergy.

The decline in the number of young clergy cannot be explained away by larger trends. It is true that the percentage of young adults in the overall population has also declined since 1985, as have the total numbers of United Methodist elders, churches, and church members. But the decline in young clergy has been proportionately far greater than any of these trends.

The number of young elders is unlikely to rebound significantly in the short term. It appears that the consistent decline in the percentage of young elders hit a low point in 2005, when it sunk to 4.69 percent. In 2006 and 2007, the percentage increased to 4.89 percent and 4.92 percent respectively. Although the decline may have bottomed out, it is unrealistic to expect that the number of young clergy will rebound significantly anytime soon. The percentage of young clergy may show improvement in coming years, but that is likely to be more the result of the total number of elders decreasing as baby boom era pastors retire in larger numbers. Increasing the number of young clergy will require sustained efforts for many years to come.

The young clergy shortage is not due primarily to attrition. The Lewis Center has concluded that the primary cause of the decline in young clergy is that too few young people are choosing to enter the profession. Evidence does not support the conclusion that large numbers of young clergy are dropping out of ministry after beginning congregational service. There is, however, some evidence that more young seminarians are choosing forms of ministry other than traditional parish ministry.

The characteristics of the young clergy population today largely reflect the dynamics of the denomination as a whole. More clergy in this generation are female than in previous generations, but, like clergy in the church at large, most young elders (67 percent) are men. Young clergy are significantly more likely to be married than their age peers in the population at large. There are more young elders in the South than in any other region. About 40 percent of young elders are serving as associate pastors, typically in larger congregations. Most of the associates are found in the Southeastern and South Central Jurisdictions where there is a higher number of large churches. About 60 percent of young elders are solo or senior pastors. Of those, 67 percent serve in small churches with average attendance of less than 100.

Young clergy register high levels of satisfaction in ministry. One of the most significant findings of the Lewis Center survey was that strikingly high percentages of young clergy are satisfied with their work, their ministry settings, their support networks, and their life circumstances. In this sense, young clergy mirror their older peers. National research has shown that clergy top the list of all other occupations in terms of job satisfaction and general happiness.

Most young clergy are doing fairly well financially, but not all. The majority of young clergy indicate that their compensation is adequate, but a significant minority of about 20 percent seems to be struggling financially. Salary levels vary significantly among elders who are under 35, and a myriad of variables can affect their financial well-being. Although there is parity in the percentage of women and men in the lowest salary brackets, young clergywomen are less likely than young clergymen to receive salaries in the higher ranges.

Increasingly young clergy are burdened by large educational debt. Sixty-three percent of young United Methodist elders entered ministry with educational debt requiring years to repay, and 12 percent say they have missed an educational loan payment because they did not have the money. Fifteen percent had seminary debt of $30,000 or more.

Most young clergy experienced their call to ministry as youth within the context of their local congregation. The factors most important to young elders in discerning their call were the desire to make a difference in the life of the church, the desire to serve others, the encouragement of clergy, their experience in a congregation, and their intellectual interest in religious and theological questions. Factors that tended to be less important were major life events (such as death or divorce), campus ministry, and counseling and spiritual direction.

The declining number of youth and young persons active in local congregations is a major reason why there are fewer young clergy. The decline in the number of young clergy since 1985 has corresponded with a 34 percent decrease in the number of high school youth in United Methodist church schools during the same period, which is one statistical indicator we have of youth involvement in congregations. The pool from which young candidates for ordained ministry are most likely to emerge is simply smaller than in the past.

Recommendations

The church must change. The issue of the quality and numbers of young people entering ordained ministry must be seen side-by-side with the quality and vitality of the church itself. The church's overall health is the most important factor determining who comes into ordained ministry. God calls at all times, and people respond to God's call. But it is more likely that God's call will be heard and accepted by more young people if the church is one in which they are active and in which God's mission to make disciples and transform the world is alive. In a society where the bulk of the population is younger and more diverse, it is not likely that a church will attract large numbers of capable young leaders until it demonstrates that it is committed to reaching more people, younger people, and more diverse people. The recruitment of new young clergy must be undertaken within the larger context of efforts to revitalize the church, its mission, and its appeal to younger generations.

Revitalize youth ministry. A critical first step in addressing the young clergy crisis is to increase the number of children and youth meaningfully involved in the church, since this is the pool from which most future young candidates for ordained ministry will emerge. Congregations must prioritize youth ministry. They must open their doors to youth in their communities, listen and respond to the spiritual needs of young people today, and engage them in meaningful leadership roles.

Cultivate call among the young. All of us in the church—local congregations, pastors, conference leaders, denominational leaders, youth ministers, campus ministers, and educators—share the important responsibility of encouraging and guiding those who seek to serve God through ordained ministry. We must all reclaim the task of the enlistment of youth and redouble our efforts. Local congregations in particular must be strengthened and encouraged in the role they play in both helping youth hear the call to ministry and in helping them respond.

Increase enlistment efforts with the understanding that these are necessary but not sufficient. Renewed enlistment efforts in the form of national and regional exploration events have proved successful in recent years. These efforts should be expanded, as should enlistment efforts by seminaries, conferences, and congregations. But we must understand that intensified enlistment efforts cannot alone solve the problem until the number of young persons in the church who might hear and respond to God's call increases.

Increase the funding of theological education. Arresting the mounting tide of educational debt among seminary graduates requires partnership. To keep tuition reasonable and provide assistance to those with greatest need, seminaries must multiply the fund-raising and development efforts that support student financial assistance, and they must ensure that assistance keeps pace with student costs. The denomination must increase its support of theological education, and conferences and individual congregations must also do their part to fund the education of future young clergy.

Make the entry process positive and formative. Conferences should examine their candidacy and ordination processes to make sure that they do not present undue stumbling blocks to young persons entering ministry. The emphasis must be on the spiritual and professional development of the candidates, rather than institutional requirements. Procedures should also be scrutinized to eliminate any subtle forms of discrimination against the young.

Rename and reframe the probationary process. The period of time between commissioning and ordination, now called probation, should be renamed to avoid the unfortunate connotations of criminal behavior and guilt. The process should be reframed to focus on its stated goal—helping candidates develop effectiveness in ministry before they are ordained.

Put mentoring front and center. All of the Lewis Center's research points to the conclusion that mentoring has more potential to develop effectiveness in those entering ministry than any other component of the entry process. Conferences should emphasize mentoring and improve it by selecting good mentors, training them well, and carefully matching them with those to be mentored.

Pay more attention to the first and second appointments young clergy receive. More strategic deployment of young clergy is arguably the best way the denomination can use the scarce resource of young leadership to enhance its outreach among younger generations while at the same time helping young clergy survive and thrive in ministry. In some cases, this will mean appointing young pastors as associates or to teaching congregations where they can develop their ministry skills. In other cases, it will mean appointing young clergy to congregations and communities where there is significant potential for reaching the young. Conferences can no longer afford to consider young clergy at the very end of the appointment process.

Review the salaries received by young clergy. Conference leaders need to be sensitive to the many variables that can affect a young pastor's financial situation and watch for signs of severe financial distress. All annual conferences should regularly reassess their entry and minimum salaries in light of local costs of living factors. They must also be aware that young clergy increasingly bear the burden of large educational debts.

Provide opportunities for young clergy to be together. Young clergy find great benefit in the experience of being together with their clergy peers. Because some districts and conferences have very few young clergy, special opportunities should be created to bring young clergy together for fellowship, mutual support, and leadership development.

Examine congregational attitudes toward younger pastors. Open minds and a welcoming spirit can go a long way toward minimizing the generational tensions that sometimes exist between older congregations and younger pastors. Church members should be reminded to treat a young clergyperson as a pastor, not as they would a child or grandchild.

Listen. Listening could be the simplest and the most effective thing that conference leaders could do to improve the world of young clergy and to make their conferences more attractive and hospitable for younger clergy. While this needs to be done on a daily basis, several conferences have recently held forums or other special events to give young clergy the opportunity to be heard. More of this is needed.

Develop young leadership. Conferences should take stock of where and how young pastors are serving in conference positions. Conference leadership structures can be examined to make sure that the young are being encouraged in leadership, not excluded. Special leadership development efforts designed for young clergy must be continued and expanded. The Lewis Fellows program and other such programs that have been developed across the country, many with help from the Lilly Endowment, Inc., have already demonstrated how important this effort is both for enhancing young clergy leadership and also for peer support.

Conclusion

Younger United Methodist pastors must walk the line between the church, theology and traditions that they cherish, and the need to create faith communities that will speak to future generations of Christians. . . . Leading the church has not ever been easy; leading on the cusp of the postmodern era will require nothing short of the leader's full calling and commitment.[1]

Amy Aitken, young pastor, California

One could argue that it is hardly a good time to celebrate ordained ministry for emerging generations. In many ways, recent years have been very difficult for clergy. But has it not always been so? Notice how clergy have been the objects of negative stereotyping in earlier generations—on television, in the news media, and even by great writers. Remember how J. D. Salinger's character Holden Caulfield complained that all the preachers he ever heard spoke in "Holy Joe" tones? He could not understand why they did not speak in their natural voices. Or recall the line from John Updike's *Rabbit, Run*, "He is getting slightly annoyed at the way the minister isn't bawling him out or something; he doesn't seem to know his job."

Unfortunately, the issues today are more serious than ministerial monotone or judgmental preaching. In these times, when integrity is a key issue in government, business, and faith communities, the church and its leaders have shown that they are not exempt from failure. Like many other public leaders, some church leaders have been discredited. Too often we have seen familiar patterns—hypocrisy, greed, failures of personal morality, and one-issue zealotry. The examples are numerous and painful. Although this is not the first era in which the integrity of religious leaders has been suspect, it is a reality today that must be taken into account.

Far less dramatic, but perhaps more devastating over the long term, is the perception that self-interest has supplanted service as the guiding mark of ministry. Too often both mainline churches and television evangelists have appeared more concerned with institutional or personal self-interest and narrow causes, whether liberal or conservative, than with the great tradition and message of Christ's church. We must acknowledge that these realities have reduced the church's capacity for leadership in our society and, at the same time, made ordained ministry less inviting.

Yet the Great Calling Still Lives

We envision a new generation of clergy leaders who can do more than provide theological rhetoric for personal and political causes. The new generation of clergy must define the reality of the human and social conditions so that personal and public transformation can emerge. Ronald F. Thiemann, former dean of Harvard Divinity School, is convinced that "the mainstream religious communities will recover their public voices only when they rediscover their own roots.... Recovery of an authentic public voice and rediscovery of religious heritage must go hand in hand."[2]

What does rediscovery of heritage mean for those called to Christian ministry today—the young, as well as their older colleagues? First, it means remembering that all ministry derives from Jesus Christ. In Jesus, we see one who came not to be served, but to serve. This spirit is reflected in the words of the John Wesley Covenant Service, "We are no longer our own, but thine." The key words for ministry are service, not security; calling, not career; mission, not profession.

Another key to recovering our heritage is remembering the importance of vital spiritual grounding and faith. Faith is contagious. It is caught, rather than learned, through ministry that preaches and believes that the blind will see and those who hate will come to love, that those who make war will come to love peace, that the humble will be exalted and the proud made humble, and that all humanity will come to know the love of God manifest in Jesus Christ.

Recovering our heritage also means identifying with a great vision. The calling to ordained ministry is a calling to be a part of a great vision. The greatness of ministry is not to be found in the church structure or in our particular assignment but in the greatness of the vision given to the people of God. Young clergy have told us that their generation seeks to be part of work that is significant, that makes a difference. Even if all the suggestions of this book for improving the situation of young clergy became a reality, there must be something more to energize a lifetime of ministry. When people feel they are a part of a great vision that has ultimate significance, there is no limit to what they can do.

Letty Russell says that as the people of God, we are called to live as if the world were as God intends, and in so doing, we help the world live its way into a new future. This is the message of the writer of Ephesians, who describes the way in which Jews and Gentiles have been made one community in the church. The church, then, is a model for what God intends for the whole world. As remarkable as this unity is, it is but a glimpse of what God intends for the whole world. It is only a sign of what can happen in the whole of creation. It is as if God is saying, "If this can happen here, among these people, there is no limit to what is possible."

How splendid it would be if the church could become that kind of model. If people wanted to see where there is perfect peace, then they could simply look at the church. Where there is justice, look at the church. Where categories of race and class that matter so much to the world mean nothing, look at the church. Where every dividing wall has been destroyed, and all are one in Christ Jesus, look at the church. Where young and old face the future together, look at the church. What a great vision we have!

No Higher Calling

We write not only as observers of United Methodist ordained ministry but also as beneficiaries of that ministry. Our lives have been blessed and shaped in innumerable ways by the faithful and fruitful ministries of United Methodist clergy. We wish that experience for more and more people in our society. The calling of God to ordained ministry is a high calling. Ministry can be the most demanding and challenging of callings. It can also be the most fulfilling and rewarding. When done poorly, it is a disgrace. When done faithfully and well, there is no higher calling.

Signs of Hope

Are young clergy better? No. But they are younger, and that does matter. Young clergy bring energy, passion, and perspectives sorely needed by The United Methodist Church today. One can make that case without idealizing the emerging generation of clergy. The hope the church places in them, and which they receive with some misgivings, is more than any generation can accomplish alone. They are not interested in being seen as saviors of the church. They are open to joining with others to shape a new church in response to a radically different cultural context.

Young clergy want their own lives to be better, but they want even more to be a part of a vital church that engages the world for Christ, transforming lives and communities. With their help, can the church retool to reach emerging generations that have grown up in a world different from that of previous generations?

One encouraging sign comes from a very unlikely source. Do you know what is reported to be the largest student gathering in the United States each year? It is the FFA. Yes, the group you may remember from high school—known in those days as the Future Farmers of America with its members in distinctive blue jackets.

Are you surprised? You should be. The FFA has reinvented itself in the midst of hard times: the number of farms in the United States has gone from seven million when the FFA began, to two million today. Farm employment as a percentage of the workforce has gone from 21 percent to less than 2 percent. The low point for the FFA came in 1992 when their membership dropped to 383,000 members. Today they have 495,000. They now have more members in towns, suburbs, and cities than in rural areas. Their largest chapter is in an urban high school in Philadelphia, Pennsylvania.

How did this transformation take place? They literally reinvented themselves around a broader vision. They expanded their focus to include the food industry, landscaping, seed, bioengineering, renewable fuels, and agricultural economics. Surely the church faces a challenging context but no more so than the FFA faced. By all odds, they should be out of existence today. If they had continued with business as usual, they would be gone today or very close to it.[3]

Young clergy did not enter ministry to preside over the demise of United Methodism. Just as they are not interested in preserving traditions for the sake of those traditions, neither are they content to accept decline as a matter of fate or a badge of honor, as they fear some current leaders in the church view things.

Humble and Hopeful

It is with hope that we conclude this book. It is a hope that the modest increases in young clergy of 2006 and 2007 (after over twenty years of uninterrupted decline) will be the first signs of a new wave of young leadership for the church. It is a hope shaped by the remarkable young clergy we have come to know, who could be investing their lives in a multitude of arenas, but who have chosen the church. It is a hope that God's spirit is stirring in ways that we must seek to join though we do not understand. If there is a new burst of energy from a new generation of pastoral leaders in the United Methodist Church, it will come of God.

Earlier, we used excerpts from Reinhold Niebuhr's journal, kept during his years as a young pastor in Detroit. Having begun the journal when he was a 23-year-old new pastor, toward the end of the volume, he writes these words about ordained ministry as a seasoned 36-year-old.

Reinhold Niebuhr
1928 (age 36)

A very sophisticated young man assured me in our discussion today . . . that no intelligent person would enter the ministry today. He was sure that the ministry was impossible as a vocation not only because too many irrationalities were still enmeshed with religion but also because there was no real opportunity for usefulness in the church. I tried to enlighten this sophomoric wise man.

Granted all the weaknesses of the church and the limitations of the ministry as a profession, where can one invest one's life where it can be made more effective in as many directions?

You can deal with children and young people and help them to set their life goals and organize their personalities around just and reasonable values.

You can help the imperiled family shape the standards and the values by which the institution of family life may be saved and adjusted to the new conditions of an industrial civilization.

You can awaken a complacent civilization to the injustices which modern industrialism is developing. . . .

You can soften the asperities of racial conflict and aid the various groups of a polyglot city to understand one another and themselves.

You can direct the thoughts and the hopes of [people] to those facts and those truths which mitigate the cruelty of the natural world and give [people] the opportunity to assert the dignity of human life in the face of the contempt of nature. . . .

Here is a task which requires the knowledge of a social scientist and the insight and imagination of a poet, the executive talents of a business [leader] and the mental discipline of a philosopher. Of course none of us meets all the demands made upon us. . . .[4]

Amy Aitken, a young pastor in California, did her doctoral work in a study of young clergy in her conference. She wrote of them and of her generation of clergy in this way:

> We move into the future surrounded by that great "cloud of witnesses" who have gone before us, facing the challenges of their day with conviction and grace. The young witnesses that I met with seemed ready, if not appropriately humbled by the task, to faithfully lead the church into God's postmodern era. We cross this bridge cautiously but with great hope, knowing that as we do, we are surrounded by God's grace, God's people, and God's call upon our lives and Christ's church.[5]

Appendix A

A Snapshot of Young Clergy Survey Responses

About the Survey

In 2007, the Lewis Center for Church Leadership conducted an online survey of United Methodist clergy under the age of 35 in the United States. The survey was conducted from March through May. Responses were received from 496 clergy in the target age group. Of those responding, 398 were elders, out of a total of 876 young elders in the denomination today, for a response rate of over 45%. The estimated response rate among young deacons was over 50% based on young deacons reported by the General Board of Pension and Health Benefits, but we know there tend to be more deacons than those who have accounts with the board. About 16 percent of young local pastors participated in the survey.

The Lewis Center developed the questions drawing upon (1) its prior knowledge of young clergy and others entering ministry; (2) input and recommendations solicited from young clergy persons, and (3) advice from other researchers.

A Snapshot of Young Clergy Survey Responses

	Total	%	Elder	%	Deacon	%	LP	%
	496	100%	398		36		60	
Gender								
Male	292	59%	240	60%	10	28%	40	67%
Female	204	41%	158	40%	26	72%	20	33%
Total Responses	496		398		36		60	
Marital Status								
Married	374	76%	310	78%	19	53%	44	73%
Single	121	24%	87	22%	17	47%	16	27%
Total Responses	495		397		36		60	
Race								
Native American	2	0%	2	1%	0	0%	0	0%
Asian/Pacific Islander	6	1%	4	1%	1	3%	1	2%
African American	8	2%	3	1%	1	3%	4	7%
Caucasian/ White	462	94%	379	96%	31	86%	50	85%
Hispanic/ Latino/ Latina	7	1%	3	1%	1	3%	3	5%
Multiracial	3	1%	3	1%	0	0%	0	0%
Other	5	1%	2	1%	2	6%	1	2%
Total Responses	493		396		36		59	
Ordination								
Deacon	36	7%						
Elder	398	81%						
Local Pastor	60	12%						
Total Responses	494							

	Total	%	Elder	%	Deacon	%	LP	%
Year in Current Appointment								
First	189	38%	139	35%	16	44%	32	54%
Second	123	25%	100	25%	9	25%	14	24%
Third	90	18%	75	19%	7	19%	8	14%
Fourth	48	10%	43	11%	1	3%	4	7%
Fifth or more	42	9%	38	10%	3	8%	1	2%
Total Responses	492		395		36		59	
Number of Congregations Served								
One	375	78%	313	80%	27	87%	33	55%
Two	84	17%	59	15%	3	10%	22	37%
Three	23	5%	17	4%	1	3%	5	8%
Total Responses	482		389		31		60	
Full- or PartTime								
Full-Time	419	86%	363	93%	30	83%	27	45%
Less than Full-Time	69	14%	28	7%	6	17%	33	55%
Total Responses	488		391		36		60	
Type of Appointment								
Solo/Senior Pastor	234	48%	193	49%	1	3%	38	63%
Associate	175	36%	154	39%	11	31%	9	15%
Campus Minister	23	5%	19	5%	3	8%	1	2%
Hospital Chaplain	1	0%	0	0%	1	3%	0	0%
Missionary	3	1%	0	0%	3	8%	0	0%
Church Planter	6	1%	5	1%	0	0%	1	2%
Educator	5	1%	3	1%	2	6%	0	0%
Student	13	3%	6	2%	0	0%	7	12%
Other	31	6%	13	3%	15	42%	4	7%
Total Responses	491		393		36		60	

	Total	%	Elder	%	Deacon	%	LP	%
What is your annual salary?								
less than $25,000	80	16%	33	9%	8	22%	37	62%
25,000 – 29,999	72	15%	56	14%	8	22%	8	13%
30,000 – 34,999	153	31%	130	34%	11	31%	12	20%
35,000 – 39,999	90	19%	82	21%	5	14%	3	5%
40,000 – 44,999	49	10%	47	12%	2	6%	0	0%
45,000 – 49,999	21	4%	21	5%	0	0%	0	0%
More than 50,000	21	4%	19	5%	2	6%	0	0%
Total Responses	486		388		36		60	
Do you have health insurance?								
Yes	449	92%	375	96%	32	89%	41	68%
No	39	8%	15	4%	4	11%	19	32%
Total Responses	482		387		35		58	
How much do you pay personally for health insurance?								
Nothing	212	44%	167	43%	18	51%	27	47%
Less than $3,000	171	35%	137	35%	12	34%	20	34%
3,000 – 5,999	66	14%	53	14%	2	6%	11	19%
6,000 – 8,999	26	5%	23	6%	3	9%	0	0%
9,000 – 11,999	4	1%	4	1%	0	0%	0	0%
12,000 – 14,999	2	0%	2	1%	0	0%	0	0%
$15,000 or more	1	0%	1	0%	0	0%	0	0%
Total Responses	482		387		35		58	

	Total	%	Elder	%	Deacon	%	LP	%
Parsonage or Housing Allowance								
Parsonage	276	61%	232	62%	9	39%	35	64%
Housing Allowance	178	39%	144	38%	14	61%	20	36%
Total Responses	454		376		23		55	
If you receive housing allowance, how much is it?								
Less than $12,000	65	35%	50	33%	4	27%	11	58%
12,000 – 17,999	88	48%	71	47%	9	60%	8	42%
18,000 – 23,999	25	14%	23	15%	2	13%	0	0%
24,000 – 29,999	4	2%	4	3%	0	0%	0	0%
$30,000 or more	2	1%	2	1%	0	0%	0	0%
Total Responses	184		150		15		19	
Under-graduate Debt								
None	243	50%	204	52%	16	44%	23	38%
Less than $5,000	29	6%	24	6%	2	6%	3	5%
5,000 – 9,999	41	8%	30	8%	5	14%	5	8%
10,000 – 14,999	58	12%	48	12%	3	8%	7	12%
15,000 – 19,999	44	9%	32	8%	5	14%	7	12%
20,000 – 24,999	31	6%	25	6%	1	3%	5	8%
25,000 – 29,999	17	3%	12	3%	2	6%	3	5%
$30,000 or more	27	6%	18	5%	2	6%	7	12%
Total Responses	490		393		36		60	

	Total	%	Elder	%	Deacon	%	LP	%
Seminary Debt								
None	147	30%	119	31%	14	39%	14	23%
Less than $5,000	31	6%	20	5%	4	11%	10	17%
5,000 – 9,999	54	11%	39	10%	3	8%	7	12%
10,000 – 14,999	46	9%	39	10%	5	14%	4	7%
15,000 – 19,999	41	8%	34	9%	1	3%	8	13%
20,000 – 24,999	50	10%	41	11%	2	6%	6	10%
25,000 – 29,999	47	10%	43	11%	2	6%	2	3%
$30,000 or more	70	14%	55	14%	5	14%	9	15%
Total Responses	486		390		36		60	

Statements on which young elders most agree (75% or more strongly agree or agree)

- ❍ I feel I am growing in my effectiveness as a pastoral leader.
- ❍ (If married) My spouse is supportive of my ministry.
- ❍ Those in my appointment would say that it is a "good fit."
- ❍ I stay connected with supportive friends and colleagues outside of family.
- ❍ I expect to be an active United Methodist clergy five years from now.
- ❍ My current appointment was open to receiving a younger pastor.
- ❍ My current appointment is helping me develop as an effective pastor.
- ❍ I feel supported by clergy colleagues.
- ❍ I feel supported by those I serve in my appointment.
- ❍ I know what is expected of me by those in my appointment.
- ❍ I am likely to recommend ordained ministry in the UMC to other young people.

Statements on which young elders most disagree (50% or more strongly disagree or disagree)

- ❍ Financial struggles hinder my ability to minister effectively.
- ❍ Around church members, I feel I have to prove myself because of my young age.
- ❍ Congregations should select their pastors from a pool of qualified clergy within their conference willing to be considered.
- ❍ The generation gap between me and the older persons with whom I work is a problem.
- ❍ Itineracy as practiced today is working well.

What aspect or aspects of the candidacy and ordination process are most encouraging for young persons?

- ❍ Mentoring (115)
- ❍ Time spent with other probationers/collegiality/relationships (60)
- ❍ Desire of the conference to have younger clergy (54)
- ❍ Clarifying and confirming my call (51)
- ❍ Support and encouragement (48)

What aspect or aspects of the candidacy and ordination process are most discouraging for young persons?

- ❍ Length of process (118)
- ❍ Felt mistreated in the process (62)
- ❍ Parts of process seeming unnecessarily bureaucratic (47)
- ❍ Unclear requirements/expectations/communication (43)

What one change in The United Methodist Church would make it more attractive for potential young clergy?

- ❍ Itineracy, appointments, and appointment systems (92)
- ❍ Ordination process (78)
- ❍ Finances (74)
- ❍ More visibility and inclusion of young clergy (48)

If you could change your appointment, what one thing would you want to be different in the new appointment?

- ❍ Different location (urban, etc.) (39)
- ❍ Openness to change and new ideas (38)
- ❍ A more active, dedicated church (24)
- ❍ More money (23)

What aspect of ministry energizes you the most?

- ❍ Preaching and sermon preparation (122)
- ❍ Worship (planning and leading, contemporary and traditional) (74)
- ❍ Discipleship (including growth in faith and transformation of lives) (66)
- ❍ Teaching (Bible study, small groups, etc.) (54)
- ❍ Mission, service, outreach, and social justice ministries (48)
- ❍ Pastoral care and visitation (43)

What aspect of ministry leaves you feeling the most drained?

- ❍ Pastoral care and visitation (92)
- ❍ Administration (83)
- ❍ Conflict (50)
- ❍ Meetings (49)
- ❍ People and attitudes (39)

What one thing could your annual conference do to be more supportive of young clergy?

- ❍ More attention to first and second appointments (54)
- ❍ Finances (51)
- ❍ Provide opportunities for young clergy to gather (49)
- ❍ Mentoring (36)

Appendix B

U.M.C.
Clergy Age Trends Report

This report builds on the first report on clergy age trends issued by the Lewis Center for Church Leadership in 2006. That report, *Clergy Age Trends in the United Methodist Church: 1985–2005*, documented the dramatic decline in United Methodist elders in both numbers and percentages over a twenty-year period. The original report is available at the Center's website. This report presents a snapshot of where clergy age trends stand in 2007.

This report contains information on elders, deacons, and local pastors in the five jurisdictional conferences of The United Methodist Church. The Lewis Center has worked with the General Board of Pension and Health Benefits of The United Methodist Church to determine age trends for United Methodist clergy.

To have comparable figures across the years for elders, the figures include not only those who have been ordained elder but also those who have been commissioned on the elder track but not yet ordained. Commissioned and ordained deacons are also included in deacon numbers. While not all clergy are in the denominational pension system, most are, and the percentage not in the system tends to stay the same across the years, thus making trend comparisons possible. Readers should keep in mind that the number of total deacons in this report is significantly lower than the number of deacons in the denomination because deacons, more than other clergy, work in employment settings with pension plans other than through the General Board. For local pastors, full-time and part-time local pastors are included, but student local pastors are excluded. Available data on clergy age trends in other denominations have been included to facilitate comparisons. Since the General Board of Pension and Health Benefits does not keep records of clergy by race, we were not able to make comparisons by racial groups.

Changes since the 2005 Report

There is modest, but good, news for United Methodists. The consistent decline in under-35 elders as a percentage of all elders hit its low point in 2005 and has held relatively steady with slight increases in 2006 and 2007. Young elders were 4.69 percent of all elders in 2005. In 2006 and 2007, the figures are 4.89 percent and 4.92 percent respectively. The actual number of young elders declined in 2007 over 2006 but still showed an increase as a percentage because of the decreasing size of the pool of elders. This trend may continue in the coming years as baby boomers retire in large numbers. Young deacons increased in percentage and numbers in both 2006 and 2007, going from 5.41 percent of all deacons in 2005 to 7.10 percent in 2007. Young local pastors declined in percentage and numbers between 2005 and 2007, going from 5.69 percent of all local pastors in 2005 to 5.48 percent in 2007.

On the other end of the age spectrum of active clergy, the greatest growth continues to occur in the 55 to 70 age cohort. This group increased from 40.90 percent in 2005 to 44.34 percent in 2007. A number of annual conferences have over 50 percent of their active elders in this category. Deacons in this older age group increased very slightly from 2006 to 2007, from 41.94 percent to 42.24 percent. Local pastors, traditionally an older group of clergy, continue to have a larger percentage between 55 and 70, going from 45.01 percent in 2005 to 48.39 percent in 2007.

The middle-age grouping, 35 to 54, has a smaller proportion of elders now than in 2005, going from 54.42 percent to 50.74. Deacons in this middle age group declined slightly from 2006 to 2007, from 51.90 percent to 50.67 percent. Middle-age local pastors declined as a proportion of all local pastors from 49.30 percent to 46.13 percent between 2005 and 2007.

The median age (half older, half younger) in 2007 for elders was 53; deacons, 51; and local pastors, 54. The average age in 2007 for elders was 53; deacons, 52; and local pastors, 53. The mode age (single age most represented) for elders in 2007 was 59; deacons, 51; and local pastors, 60.

In terms of other denominations, we have limited historical data, but there are some for which we have data for more than one year. More denominations participated in this 2007 report so more comparisons should be possible in future reports. Of those denominations for which we have data for more than one year, joining The United Methodist Church in showing increases in young clergy as a percentage of total clergy was the Evangelical Lutheran Church in America, which went from 4.86 percent in 2005 to 5.92 percent in 2007. Young clergy in the Church of the Nazarene declined from 12.72 percent in 2006 to 10.68 percent in 2007, though they continue to have a higher percentage of young clergy than most denominations. The Presbyterian Church (U.S.A.) showed a decline from 7.10 percent in 2002 to 6.20 percent in 2007, though this is a modest decline for a five-year period, and they continue to have the strongest cohort of under-35 clergy of the traditional mainline churches. Other denominations showing proportionate declines in young clergy are the American Baptist (from 5.50 percent in 2006 to 5.10 percent in 2007) and the Episcopal Church (from 4.10 percent in 2006 to 3.43 percent in 2007).

In addition to the information provided in this report, readers may find additional information, including additional conference by conference breakdowns, by going to the Lewis Center website at www.churchleadership.com.

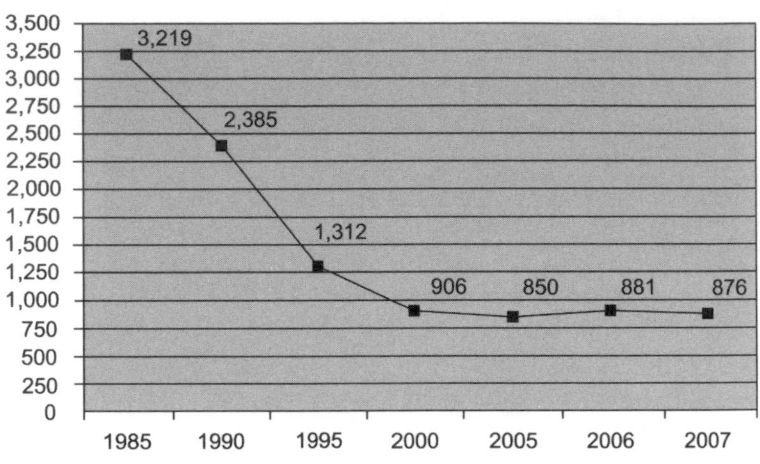
Number of UMC Elders Under 35
3,500
3,250
3,000
2,750
2,500
2,250
2,000
1,750
1,500
1,250
1,000
750
500
250
0
3,219
2,385
1,312
906
850
881
876
1985
1990
1995
2000
2005
2006
2007

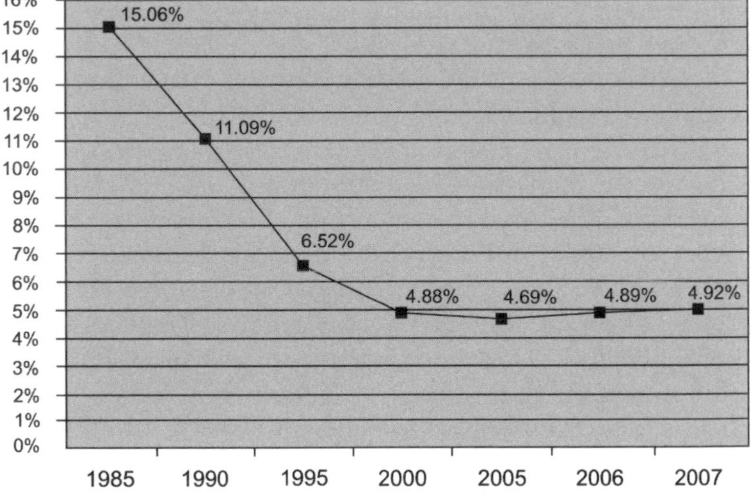
Percentage of UMC Elders Under 35
16%
15%
14%
13%
12%
11%
10%
9%
8%
7%
6%
5%
4%
3%
2%
1%
0%
15.06%
11.09%
6.52%
4.88%
4.69%
4.89%
4.92%
1985
1990
1995
2000
2005
2006
2007

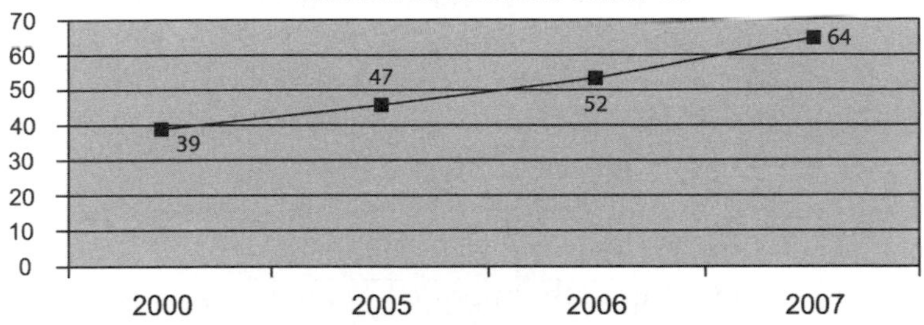
Number of Deacons Under 35
70
60
50
40
30
20
10
0
39
47
52
64
2000
2005
2006
2007

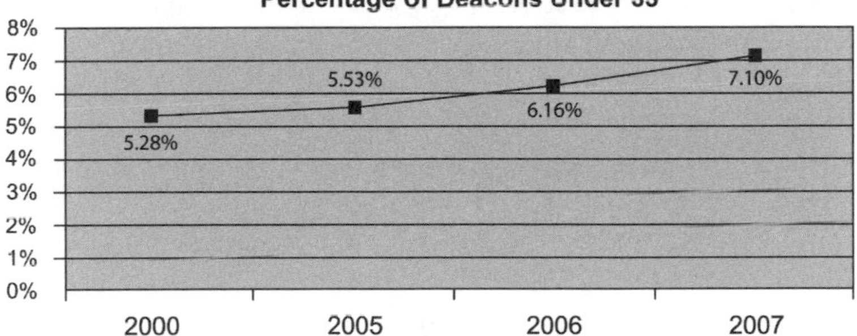
Percentage of Deacons Under 35
8%
7%
6%
5%
4%
3%
2%
1%
0%
5.28%
5.53%
6.16%
7.10%
2000
2005
2006
2007

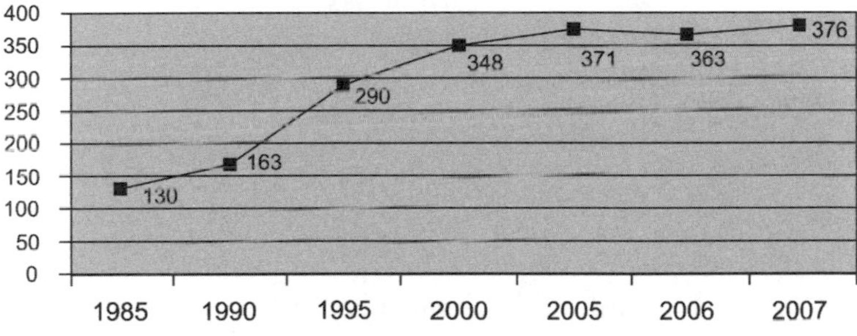
Number of Local Pastors Under 35
400
350
300
250
200
150
100
50
0
130
163
290
348
371
363
376
1985
1990
1995
2000
2005
2006
2007

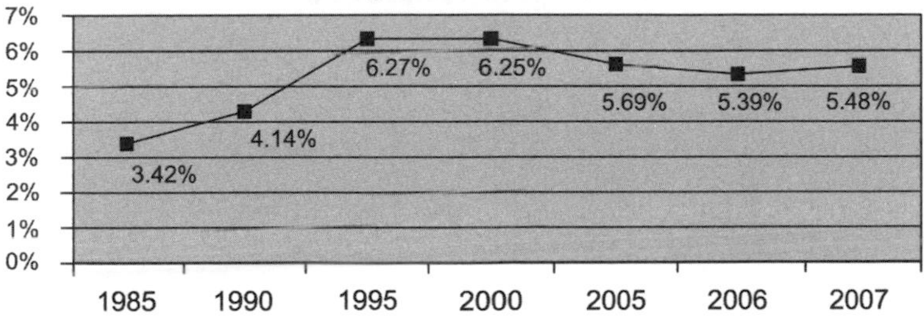
Percentage of Local Pastors Under 35
7%
6%
5%
4%
3%
2%
1%
0%
3.42%
4.14%
6.27%
6.25%
5.69%
5.39%
5.48%
1985
1990
1995
2000
2005
2006
2007

About the Lewis Center for Church Leadership

The Lewis Center for Church Leadership was established in 2003 by Wesley Theological Seminary in Washington, D.C., to advance the understanding of Christian leadership and promote the faithful and fruitful practice of Christian leadership in the church and in society. The Center is building a vision for church leadership grounded in faith, informed by knowledge, and exercised in effective action. It seeks a holistic understanding of Christian leadership that brings together theology and management, scholarship and practice, research and application.

The Lewis Center serves as a resource for seminary students, lay and clergy congregational leaders, and denominational officials. Through teaching, research, publications, and training, the Lewis Center supports visionary spiritual leaders and addresses those key leadership issues that are crucial to the church's witness. The Center seeks to be a trusted resource for church leadesrhip, helping congregations and denominations serve, thrive, and grow.

For more information or to subscribe to the Center's free online newsletter, *Leading Ideas*, go to:

www.churchleadership.com

Lewis Center for Church Leadership
Wesley Theological Seminary
4500 Massachusetts Ave., NW
Washington, DC 20016

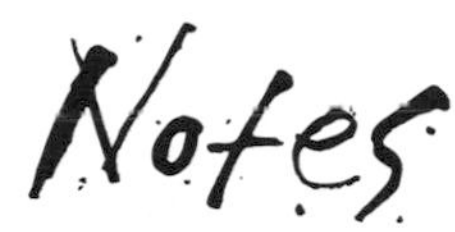

Introduction

1. John R. Mott, *The Future Leadership of the Church* (New York: YMCA, 1908), 4.
2. Amy Aitken, "Together on the Edge: A Covenant Group of Younger Pastors Exploring the Spiritual, Theological, and Practical Issues of Leading the United Methodist Church into the Postmodern Era" (D.Min. Project Thesis, Wesley Theological Seminary, 2006), 41.
3. James MacGregor Burns, *Leadership* (New York: Harper & Row, 1978), 1.

1. Dimensions of the Young Clergy Crisis

1. Lovett H. Weems, Jr., *Clergy Age Trends in the United Methodist Church: 1985-2005*. Lewis Center for Church Leadership, 2006.
2. Sources of clergy age data for denominations other than the United Methodist Church are as follows: American Baptist Churches USA, Ministers and Missionaries Benefit Board; Assemblies of God, Statistician's Office; Christian Church (Disciples of Christ), Pension Fund; Church of God (Anderson, Indiana); the Board of Pensions Church of the Nazarene, Pensions and Benefits USA; Episcopal Church, Church Pension Fund; Evangelical Lutheran Church in America (ELCA), Department of Research & Evaluation; Lutheran Church (Missouri Synod), Concordia Plan Services; Presbyterian Church (U.S.A.), Board of Pensions; Reform Judaism, Reform Pension Board; Roman Catholic (No central office keeps information

on Catholic priests' ages, researchers at Catholic Univeresity did a survey of American priests in 2001 from which these figures come. The survey had a high response rate of 71%. Dean R. Hoge and Jacqueline E. Wenger, "Evolving Visions of the Priesthood," *Liturgical Press*, 2003, p. 200); Seventh Day Adventist Church, Adventist Retirement Plan; United Church of Canada, Ministry and Employment Services Unit.

3. Barbara G. Wheeler, "Is There a Problem? Theological Students and Religious Leadership for the Future." *Auburn Studies* 8, (July 2001): 17.

4. Neela Banerjee, "Students Flock to Seminaries, but Fewer See Pulpit in Future," *New York Times*, March 17, 2006.

5. Ibid.

6. Information provided by Barbara G. Wheeler from forthcoming research to be published by the Center for the Study of Theological Education, Auburn Theological Seminary.

7. L. Jackson Brown, *Adequacy of Current and Future Dental Workforce: Theory and Analysis* (American Dental Association, 2004), 98.

8. Barbara G. Wheeler, "Is There a Problem? Theological Students and Religious Leadership for the Future," *Auburn Studies* 8 (July 2001): 5.

2. A Profile of Today's Young Clergy

1. Reinhold Niebuhr, *Leaves from the Notebook of a Tamed Cynic* (Louisville, Ky.: Westminster John Knox Press, reissue 1991 [1929]), 9.

2. Sam Roberts, "To Be Married Means to Be Outnumbered," *New York Times*, 15 October, 2006.

3. Ibid.

4. Tom W. Smith, "Job Satisfaction in the United States." Published April 17, 2007 by the National Opinion Research Center of the University of Chicago.

3. Why Young Clergy Matter

1. New York State Education Department, Office of the Professions website, www.op.nysed.gov.

2. C. Kirk Hadaway and Penny L. Marler, "New Church Development: A Research Report" (N.Y.: Office of Research, Episcopal Church Center, 2001), 13.

3. Barbara G. Wheeler, "Is There a Problem? Theological Students and Religious Leadership for the Future," *Auburn Studies*, 8 (July 2001): 16-17.

4. Ibid., 15-16.

5. Jay A. Conger and Beth Benjamin, *Building Leaders: How Successful Companies Develop the Next Generation* (San Francisco: Jossey-Bass, 1999), 261-62.

6. Donald Capps, *Young Clergy: A Biographical-Developmental Study* (Binghamton, N.Y.: Haworth Pastoral Press, 2005), 217.

7. General Board of Pension and Health Benefits of the United Methodist Church.

8. Survey taken at the annual meeting of the Church Benefits Association, San Diego, California, November 29, 2006. The CBA is comprised of pension and health professionals from approximately fifty religious denominations and organizations in the United States.

4. The Need for Enlistment

1. Data on the enrollment of women and people of color provided by the Association of Theological Schools in the United States and Canada.

2. Kevin Spears, editor, *Cultures of Call: Exploring Vocational Habits and Practices in Congregations*, Fund for Theological Education, 1:1-4.

3. W. W. Moore, Inaugural Address, Union Theological Seminary, Richmond, Vir., May 9, 1905.

5. The Importance of Youth Ministry

1. Erika Gara, "Endangered Species: Church" blog, http://endangeredspecieschurch.blogspot.com, February 1, 2007.

2. Joseph P. O'Neill and Jerilee Grandy, "The Image of Ministry: Attitudes of Young Adults Toward Organized Religion and Religious Professions," *Ministry Research Notes* (Princeton, N.J.: Educational Testing Service), Summer, (1994): 18.

3. Ibid., 3.

4. Graham Reside, "Modeling the Way: Vocational Development at Grantham Church," *Cultures of Call: Exploring Vocational Habits and Practices in Congregations*, Fund for Theological Education, 1:1.

5. Marta W. Aldrich, "State of the Church Report Encourages Dialogue" *United Methodist News Service*, June 1, 2007. http://www.umc.org (accessed June 21, 2007). The report is based in part upon research commissioned by the Connectional Table, a representative body formed at the 2004 General Conference whose responsibilities included the development of such a report.

6. Ann A. Michel, "Making Church Matter for Youth," *Leading Ideas*, online newsletter of the Lewis Center for Church Leadership, www.churchleadership.com, July 6, 2005.

7. Carol E. Lytch, *Choosing Church: What Makes a Difference for Teens* (Louisville, Ky.: Westminster John Knox Press, 2003), 25.

8. Kenda Creasy Dean, *Practicing Passion: Youth and the Quest for a Passionate Church* (New York: Zondervan, 2006), 54-56.

9. *Cultures of Call*, p. 8.

10. Mayerene Barker, "Methodists Seek Ways to Attract Young Clergy," *Circuit West*, California-Pacific Conference, July 2006.

11. Ibid.

12. Source: Fund for Theological Education.

6. The Entry Process

1. Lovett H. Weems Jr., *The Journey from Readiness to Effectiveness: An Ongoing Survey of the Probationary Process in the United Methodist Church*, Second Edition, 2005, p. 21.

2. Karen G. Puckett, "SWF, 26, Seeks UM Ordination," blog of Bethquick.com, http://bethquick.blogspot.com/, August 1, 2006.

7. The Need to Support Young Clergy

1. Andrew C. Thompson, "Gen-X Clergy Struggle Against Spiritual Isolation," *United Methodist Reporter*, September 8, 2006. (http://www.umportal.org/ (accessed July 10, 2007).

2. Amy Aitken "Together on the Edge: A Covenant Group of Younger Pastors Exploring the Spiritual, Theological, and Practical

Issues of Leading the United Methodist Church into the Postmodern Era," (D.Min. Project, Wesley Theological Seminary, 2006), 45.

3. Ann A. Michel, "Young Clergy Speak," *Circuit Rider*, March/April 2006, 9.

4. Amy Aitken, "Together on the Edge," 3.

8. Deployment of Young Clergy

1. Reinhold Niebuhr, *Leaves from the Notebook of a Tamed Cynic* (Louisville, Ky.: Westminster John Knox Press, 1980), 9.

2. Lyle E. Schaller, *Small Congregation, Big Potential: A Denominational Perspective* (Nashville: Abingdon Press, 2003), 190.

3. Lyle E. Schaller, *A Mainline Turnaround: Strategies for Congregations and Denominations* (Nashville: Abingdon Press, 2005), 91-92. As with so many things, efforts designed to help young clergy are really those things that will help everyone.

9. The Adequacy of Salaries

1. Peter Cammarano, "Padre Complex", http://www.padrecomplex.org/, November 19, 2006.

2. B. J. Bergfalk, "Naked Religion," http://www.nakedreligion.com/, October 17, 2005.

3. "Tax-Day Stress Can Put Americans' Health at Risk," *APA Help Center*, www.apahelpcenter.org (accessed June 26, 2007).

10. The Challenge of Educational Debt

1. Anthony Ruger, Sharon L. Miller, and Kim Maphis Early, "The Gathering Storm: The Educational Debt of Theological Students," *Auburn Studies* 12 (September 2005): 1-7, 22.

2. Ibid.

3. Ibid., 3.

4. Ibid., 5.

5. Ibid., 6-7.

6. Ibid., 22.

11. Bridging the Generation Gap

1. Charles Handy, *The Age of Paradox* (Boston: Harvard Business School Press, 1994), 37. Quoted in Eddie Gibbs, *Leadership Next: Changing Leaders in a Changing Culture* (Downers Grove, Ill.: InterVarsity Press, 2005) 53.

2. Erika Gara, "Endangered Species: Church" blog, http://endangeredspeiceschurch.blogspot.com, December 19, 2006.

3. Amy Aitken, "Together on the Edge: A Covenant Group of Younger Pastors Exploring the Spiritual, Theological, and Practical Issues of Leading the United Methodist Church into the Postmodern Era," (D.Min. Project Thesis, Wesley Theological Seminary, 2006), 47.

4. Brian McLaren, "Unless We Become Humble People," *Circuit Rider*, March/April 2006, 15.

5. Ann A. Michel, "Young Clergy Speak," *Circuit Rider*, March/April 2006, 10.

6. Aitken, "Together on the Edge," 48.

7. Eddie Gibbs, *Leadership Next: Changing Leaders in a Changing Culture* (Downers Grove, Ill.: InterVarsity Press, 2005), 53.

8. Ron A. Carucci, *Leadership Divided: What Emerging Leaders Need and What You Might Be Missing* (San Francisco: Jossey-Bass, 2006), 17.

9. Henri Nouwen, *Return of the Prodigal Son* (New York: Doubleday, 1992), 131-32.

10. Jennifer J. Deal, *Retiring the Generation Gap: How Employees Young and Old Can Find Common Ground* (San Francisco: Jossey-Bass, 2007), 21-22

11. Ibid., 31-36.

12. Lovett H. Weems Jr., *Take the Next Step: Leading Lasting Change in the Church* (Nashville: Abingdon Press, 2003), chapter 1.

12. The Church Must Change

1. Ronald F. Thiemann, "Toward the Integrated Study of Religion," *Harvard Divinity Bulletin* 21:4 (1992): 15.

2. *Perspective*, Perkins School of Theology (Winter, 1993): 11-12.

3. Kenneth L. Woodward, "The High Priest of Scholarship," *Newsweek*, August 7, 1989, 52.

4. Leander Keck, *The Church Confident* (Nashville: Abingdon Press, 1993), 93.